WORDPERFECT® 5.1

Sarah E. Hutchinson
Stacey C. Sawyer
Glen J. Coulthard

THE IRWIN ADVANTAGE SERIES
FOR COMPUTER EDUCATION
♦

IRWIN

Burr Ridge, Illinois
Boston, Massachusetts
Sydney, Australia

Printed in the United States of America.

ISBN 0-256-13478-2

WordPerfect® is a registered trademark of WordPerfect Corporation.

5 6 7 8 9 0 ML 0 9 8 7 6 5 4 3

CONTENTS

SESSION 1
WORDPERFECT FUNDAMENTALS   1

SESSION 2
FORMATTING COMMANDS   41

SESSION 3
EDITING AND PROOFING A DOCUMENT   75

SESSION 4
PRINTING AND FILE-MANAGEMENT COMMANDS   103

SESSION 5
ADVANCED FEATURES   135

USING THIS GUIDE

This tutorial is one in a series of learning guides that lead you through the most popular microcomputer software programs available. Concepts, skills, and procedures are grouped into session topics and are presented in a logical and structured manner. Commands and procedures are introduced using hands-on examples, and you are encouraged to perform the steps along with the guide. Although you may turn directly to a later session, be aware that some sessions require, or at least assume, that you have completed the previous sessions. For maximum benefit, you should work through the short-answer and hands-on exercises appearing at the end of each session.

The exercises and examples in this guide use several standard conventions to indicate menu instructions, keystroke combinations, and command instructions.

MENU INSTRUCTIONS

When you need to execute a command from a menu, the tutorial's instruction line uses a comma to separate the menu options. For example, the command for changing margins is shown as:

CHOOSE: Line, Margins

This instruction tells you to press the L key to choose the Line option and then press the M key to choose the Margins option. Keys separated by commas are not pressed at the same time.

KEYSTROKES AND KEYSTROKE COMBINATIONS

When you must press two keys together, the tutorial's instruction line shows the keys joined with a plus sign (+). For example, to use the FORMAT command in WordPerfect, hold down (Shift) and then press (F8). The instruction for using the FORMAT command is shown as:

PRESS: (Shift)+(F8)

Once both keys have been pressed, they are then immediately released.

COMMAND INSTRUCTIONS

This guide indicates with a special typeface data that you are required to type in yourself. For example:

TYPE: `George Washington`

When you are required to enter unique information, such as the current date or your name, the instructions appear in italics. The following instruction directs you to type your name in place of the actual words: "your name."

TYPE: *your name*

Instructions that use general directions rather than a specific option or command name appear italicized in the regular typeface.

SELECT: *the cursor-movement keys to highlight the print range*

WORDPERFECT® 5.1

SESSION 1

WORDPERFECT FUNDAMENTALS

You begin typing a letter. Perhaps you're an expert typist, perhaps not. You pay close attention, think you've done well, finish the task—and then you check your work, hoping to see no mistakes. No such luck. You have to start all over again. So much for your good mood.

But that's only if you used a simple typewriter. Using a computer and word processing software such as WordPerfect, you're still close to success. This session teaches you to write, edit, save, retrieve, and print WordPerfect text.

PREVIEW

When you have completed this session, you will be able to:

Describe the document cycle.
·
Create a document.
·
Save and retrieve a document.
·
Edit a document and reveal codes.
·
Print a document.

Why Is This Session Important?
Overview of WordPerfect
    Entering Text
    Editing Text
    Spell-Checking and the Thesaurus
    Formatting
    Printing
    Merging
Loading WordPerfect
The WordPerfect Screen
Using the Function Keys
Using the Pull-Down Menus
    Using a Mouse
The Cancel Key (`F1`)
Using Help (`F3`)
Creating a Document
    Inserting Text: Insert Versus Typeover
    Deleting Text: Delete Versus Backspace
    Word Wrap
Saving Your Work
    Saving a Document (`F10`)
    Saving a Document More Than Once (`F10`)
Beginning a New Document (`F7`)
Retrieving Your Files
    Retrieving a Document: You Know the
        Filename (`Shift`+`F10`)
    Retrieving a Document: You've Forgotten the
        Filename (`F5`)
Cursor-Movement Commands
Editing a Document
    Breaking One Paragraph into Two
    Inserting Text and Deleting Text
    Adding Text to the Bottom of the Document
Revealing Codes (`Alt`+`F3`) or (`F11`)
Saving the Revised Document Under a Different
   Name
Printing a Document (`Shift`+`F7`)
Exiting WordPerfect
Summary
    Command Summary
Key Terms
Exercises
    Short Answer
    Hands-On

WHY IS THIS SESSION IMPORTANT?

As more microcomputers are being used in the business workplace, more word processing software programs are being written for them. **Word processing software** allows you to create, edit, format, store and retrieve, and print documents using a computer. Bookstore and computer store shelves are full of books on different microcomputer word processing software packages. Software reviewers often judge WordPerfect to be one of the best word processing programs available for use today. In this session, we provide an overview of the different features WordPerfect provides and lead you through creating a document.

Before using an applications software package, make sure that your computer meets all the necessary hardware requirements to run the software—these **system requirements** are usually listed on the front of the applications package. To use WordPerfect on your computer you must have at least 384 K of RAM (random access memory). It's best that your computer have a hard disk, because all the WordPerfect program files and tutorial files take up 4.5 MB of disk storage. However, you can use WordPerfect on a system with two diskette drives as long as each drive has a minimum capacity of 720 K.

Before proceeding, make sure the following are true:

1. You have access to WordPerfect 5.1.

2. Your Advantage Diskette is inserted in the drive. You will save your work onto the diskette and retrieve the files that have been created for you. (Note: The Advantage Diskette can be made by copying all the files off your instructor's Master Advantage Diskette onto a formatted diskette.)

OVERVIEW OF WORDPERFECT

Each of WordPerfect's features can be used in one or more parts of the document cycle. The **document cycle** using word processing software includes the following activities: (1) entering, (2) editing, (3) spell-checking and using a thesaurus, (4) formatting, (5) saving and retrieving, and (6) printing a document. A seventh stage—merging text from separate documents into a single document—may also be part of the cycle. Each step in the document cycle uses a number of WordPerfect features.

ENTERING TEXT

After you load WordPerfect into RAM (which you will do later in this session), the next step is to enter, or key in, your text. When entering text, you will use (1) cursor movement, (2) word wrap and the (Enter) key, and (3) scrolling.

The **cursor** is a blinking or highlighted line (or block), about as wide as a character, that marks where the next character or space will be entered or where the next command operation will start. As you type a character, the cursor moves to the right. When you are editing text, you can control where the cursor is positioned by using the cursor-movement keys on your keyboard.

Another important feature of computer-based word processing is **word wrap.** When you are writing on a typewriter, to begin typing another line, you hit the carriage return or press (Enter) when the print mechanism hits the right-hand margin so that it will return to the left-hand margin. When using a computer and word processing software, you don't have to do anything at the end of a line. When the cursor reaches the right-hand margin it automatically returns to the left-hand margin of the line below. In other words, the cursor wraps around to start a new line when it reaches the right margin. If a word is being typed in that is too long to fit on the current line, the cursor will automatically move it to the next line.

Entering text almost always involves **scrolling**—the automatic movement of blocks of text up or down the screen. Many, if not most, of the documents you create will be too large to see all at once on the screen. The most you can view on your monitor is 24 to 25 lines of text; 80 characters can fit across the width of the screen. What happens when you're entering a document that is longer than 25 lines? Your document will move up, or scroll, off the top of the screen. Your screen acts like a window through which you see portions of the text you have entered. To see the portions of text that have scrolled off the screen, you need to move the cursor to the portions of text you want to see (you will learn how to do this shortly). To see a document that is longer than 25 lines in its entirety, you must print it out.

The cursor-movement keys ((↑), (↓), (←), (→)) move the cursor through your document on the screen. In addition, (PgUp) moves the cursor to the first line on the previous page, and (PgDn) moves the cursor to the first line on the next page. In this session, we describe a number of methods for moving the cursor efficiently throughout a document. These methods can save you time, especially when working on long documents.

EDITING TEXT

Let's say you've used WordPerfect to create a letter to send to a potential employer. After reviewing it, you decide to improve the letter by making changes to, or **editing,** it. A number of features can be used to edit a document. Two of the most important involve inserting and deleting text. With word processing software, all you have to do to insert text in or delete text from a document is move the cursor to the location where you want to start the operation and then press the appropriate keys. In this way, for example, you could position the cursor in the middle of a paragraph, and then insert a sentence. Once you've performed the desired operation, WordPerfect will automatically reformat your text to fit within the margins. In this session, you will practice inserting and deleting text.

Another convenient editing feature of WordPerfect is the ability to perform **block operations.** For example, what if you decide to move the first paragraph in your document to the end of your document? By using block operations, you can move, delete, and copy sentences, paragraphs, and pages by telling the software where the beginning and end points are of the block of text you want to move. Once you have defined the block of text, you issue the appropriate command to either move, delete, or copy it. WordPerfect also allows you to create a separate file out of a block of text. This feature lets you save parts of documents you will use again and again and incorporate them into new documents.

WordPerfect can also search for and replace text in a document. For instance, perhaps you used the name John instead of Jack in many places throughout your document. If your document is 20 pages long, it would take a long time to find each occurrence of "John," delete it, and type "Jack." With the **search and replace** capability, you tell the software what word or phrase you want to search for and what word or phrase you would like to replace it with. Then say goodbye to John and hello to Jack.

SPELL-CHECKING AND THE THESAURUS

WordPerfect can check for spelling errors in your document. It's amazing how many errors the spelling checker finds even after you've looked for them yourself. When you choose the menu option to check the spelling of your document, the spelling dictionary (which accompanies WordPerfect) is loaded into RAM. The words in your document are then compared to the words in the dictionary. The **spelling checker** flags each word in your document that it can't find a match for in the dictionary. For most flagged words, WordPerfect provides a list of suggested correct spellings—you have the option of choosing one to be inserted into your document in place of the incorrectly spelled word.

For example, in Figure 1.1, the spelling checker is highlighting the word "becuase" since it considers it to be misspelled. On the bottom half of the screen is a list of suggested correct spellings. In this case, you would type A to replace the incorrect spelling (becuase) with the correct spelling (because). If the speller doesn't come up with any suggested spellings, you have the option of editing the word directly. Sometimes, if the dictionary doesn't contain a word like the one you typed—for instance, someone's last name—WordPerfect will flag it even though it may be spelled correctly; WordPerfect allows you to skip these. WordPerfect also lets you add words to the dictionary, which is very useful if you use special terminology in your profession or if you must often use proper names in your documents. If you don't add these words to the dictionary, it will flag them as misspelled every time you spell-check your document. You will use the spelling checker in Session 3.

Figure 1.1

The Spelling
Checker

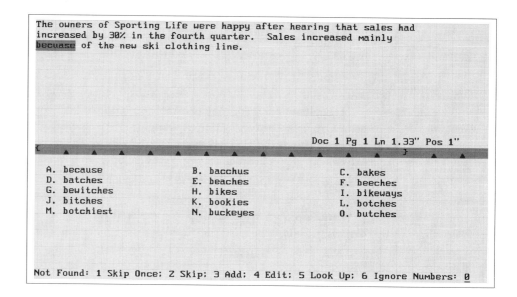

WordPerfect can also identify words with similar meanings through use of a computer-based **thesaurus.** The user simply highlights a word to be looked up and then activates the thesaurus. Words of similar meaning in the thesaurus will then be listed on the screen. For example, in Figure 1.2 the thesaurus is highlighting the word *happy.* On the bottom of the screen, the thesaurus has listed words that have similar meaning. This feature is useful when you know what you want to say but can't find the right words, or if you use the same word over and over in a document and want some alternatives. You will use the THESAURUS command in Session 3.

FORMATTING

Formatting commands, which are described in more detail in Session 2, enable you to improve the appearance of your documents, and can be viewed as falling into three categories. **Character formatting commands** enable you to perform such tasks as underlining, boldfacing, and centering. **Page formatting commands** enable you to perform such tasks as including hard page breaks, changing line spacing, changing the tab settings, and indenting. **Document formatting commands** enable you to change the size of the margins that will appear on the printed page, specify an alternate paper size, and include page numbers, headers and footers. **Headers** and **footers** contain descriptive information that appears at the top or bottom of every page. They generally contain such information as page number, date, and document title. Although defined from within the program, headers and footers appear only on your printed output, not on the screen. Figure 1.3 shows WordPerfect's Format menu.

Figure 1.2

The Thesaurus

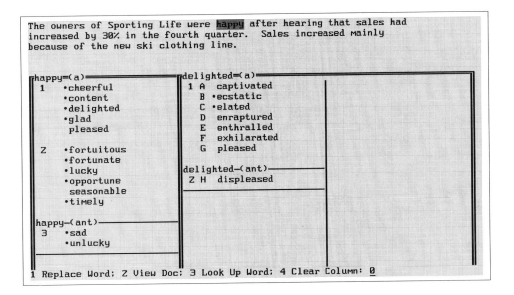

Figure 1.3

The Format menu

```
Format

   1 - Line
            Hyphenation                        Line Spacing
            Justification                      Margins Left/Right
            Line Height                        Tab Set
            Line Numbering                     Widow/Orphan Protection

   2 - Page
            Center Page (top to bottom)        Page Numbering
            Force Odd/Even Page                Paper Size/Type
            Headers and Footers                Suppress
            Margins Top/Bottom

   3 - Document
            Display Pitch                      Redline Method
            Initial Codes/Font                 Summary

   4 - Other
            Advance                            Overstrike
            Conditional End of Page            Printer Functions
            Decimal Characters                 Underline Spaces/Tabs
            Language                           Border Options

Selection: 0
```

You may in advance format your document or wait until you have finalized its content.

PRINTING

Once you've created a document and are pleased with it, you'll probably want to print the document. Printing a document involves connecting your printer to your computer, turning the printer on, and then issuing the command to print your document.

WordPerfect provides you with a number of print options. For example, when you initiate the PRINT command you can specify whether to print the entire document or just the page that the cursor is positioned on. In addition, you can specify that you want to print more than one copy of your document. WordPerfect also enables you to view your document on the screen as it will appear when printed. This feature makes it possible to see the overall effect of your formatting changes (for example, margin changes) without having to print the document out.

MERGING

Think of how much time you would save if you could send out 50 personalized cover letters to potential employers in less than an hour! Word processing software can help you do this by enabling you to bring information from two files together, which is referred to as **merging**. We lead you through the process of merging in Session 5.

LOADING WORDPERFECT

We assume that you have booted your computer with DOS (if you're not familiar with the process of loading DOS, ask your instructor).

1. WordPerfect is probably loaded in a subdirectory (named something like \WP or \WP51) on the hard disk. You may be able to load WordPerfect without making the WordPerfect subdirectory current using the CD command. To see if this is the case, type the following after the system prompt:
    TYPE: wp
    PRESS: [Enter]
    If a message such as "Bad Command or Filename" is displaying on the screen, proceed with Steps 2–3. Otherwise, skip Steps 2–3.

2. Use the CD command to make the WordPerfect subdirectory the current subdirectory. For example, if the WordPerfect subdirectory is called \WP, you would type CD\WP to accomplish this.

3. To load WordPerfect:
    TYPE: wp
    PRESS: [Enter]

THE WORDPERFECT SCREEN

What do you see? In the upper left-hand corner of the page, the cursor is blinking and waiting for you to enter text; think of your screen as a blank piece of paper. In the bottom right-hand corner of the page, you should see status information that (among other things that we'll cover later) tells what position ("Pos") the cursor is in. Note that your cursor is on line (Ln) 1, meaning the line 1 inch from the top of the paper, and in position (Pos) 1. Unless you issue a command to change the margins in your document, WordPerfect will print your document with 1-inch margins on all sides of your document (top, bottom, left, and right); by default, WordPerfect sets 1-inch margins on all sides of your document. (The term *default* refers to the assumptions made by a software program; in other words, default values are what you get unless you enter specific values of your own choosing.) Figure 1.4 shows the initial WordPerfect screen.

Figure 1.4

This screen displays after you load WordPerfect.

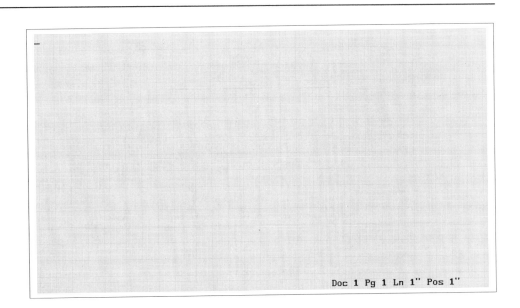

Doc 1 Pg 1 Ln 1" Pos 1"

But before we actually exercise your typing skills, we'd like to familiarize you with how to access WordPerfect's commands.

USING THE FUNCTION KEYS

WordPerfect provides the user with 40 function key commands that are accessed by holding down the Alternate ((Alt)), (Shift), or Control ((Ctrl)) keys while pressing a function key (function keys have the letter F and a number). Each function key command invokes either a command or displays a menu from which you can issue commands or display additional submenus. Figure 1.5 shows the 40 WordPerfect function key commands.

Figure 1.5

The WordPerfect function key template

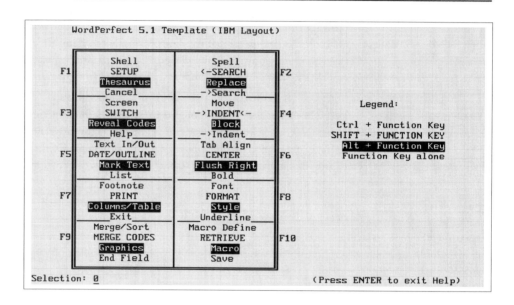

For easy reference, WordPerfect supplies each user with a template that fits around the function keys and identifies the different tasks each key performs. The template description in Figure 1.5 is intended to be used with the (F1) – (F10) function keys when they are located on the left side of the keyboard. Templates are also available from WordPerfect that are designed to work with the function keys when they are positioned horizontally across the top of the keyboard.

Note: On the template you are using, four commands are listed on each function key, each in a different color. To perform commands printed in black, simply press the function key corresponding to your choice. To perform commands printed in green, hold (Shift) down and press the appropriate function key. To perform commands printed in blue, hold (Alt) down and press the appropriate function key. Finally, to perform commands printed in red, hold (Ctrl) down and press the appropriate function key.

USING THE PULL-DOWN MENUS

Pull-down menus provide the user with an alternative method for issuing commands. The menu bar can be displayed on the top of the screen by holding (Alt) down and typing the plus (+) sign, and then typing the equal sign. Each option in the menu bar corresponds to a different pull-down menu. In Figure 1.6, the File pull-down menu is displaying in the menu bar.

Figure 1.6

The File pull-down menu

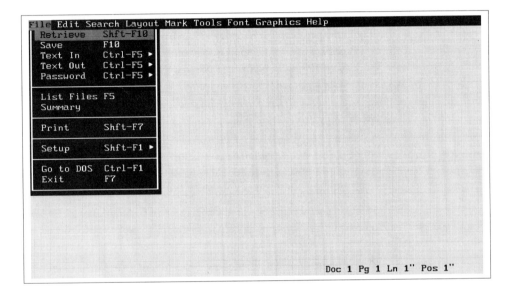

To display a pull-down menu, either highlight the menu option on the menu bar and press (Enter), or type the first letter of the menu bar option. To choose an option within a pull-down menu, either type the highlighted character, or highlight the desired option and press (Enter). Once you choose a command, WordPerfect will either issue a command or display a submenu from which you can choose a command or display additional submenus.

USING A MOUSE

To display the menu bar using a mouse, press the right button on the mouse. To display a pull-down menu, move the cursor to the desired menu bar option and then press the left mouse button. To select an option within a pull-down menu, move the cursor to the desired option, and then press the left mouse button. To exit from a menu, press the right mouse button.

Two keys can help you solve many problems in word processing, so let's look at them before you start to type.

THE CANCEL KEY (F1)

The **Cancel key** (F1) has two purposes. First, it enables you to cancel out of a command. If you have initiated a command, and decide you don't want to use it, you can cancel it by pressing F1. Second, it enables you to restore deleted text. If you are viewing your document on the screen (that is, you aren't viewing a menu) and press F1, WordPerfect displays on the screen the text you last deleted and provides you with the option of restoring to your document the deleted text. WordPerfect also gives you the option of viewing your second-to-last deletion and restoring it to your document.

Quick Reference
Cancel F1

If you are viewing a menu on the screen, this command cancels the current command. If you are viewing a document on the screen, this command enables you to restore text you have previously deleted.

USING HELP (F3)

The **Help key** (F3) provides information about any WordPerfect command. To initiate the HELP command, simply press F3. If you press F3 again, the WP template will display (Figure 1.5). Information about how to use Help will display on the screen (Figure 1.7). To obtain information about a particular function key, simply press the appropriate function key (Figure 1.8). Or if you want to determine what keystrokes will enable you to change margins, for example, simply type M and the keystroke information will appear on the screen (Figure 1.9). Or type I to obtain keystroke information about indenting. Pressing Enter or the space bar exits you out of the HELP command.

Figure 1.7

The HELP
command
was initiated
by pressing
[F3].

```
Help              License #:  WP1999255        WP 5.1   03/30/90

     Press any letter to get an alphabetical list of features.

          The list will include the features that start with that letter,
          along with the name of the key where the feature is found.  You
          can then press that key to get a description of how the feature
          works.

     Press any function key to get information about the use of the key.

          Some keys may let you choose from a menu to get more information
          about various options.  Press HELP again to display the template.




Selection: 0                                (Press ENTER to exit Help)
```

Figure 1.8

Retrieving infor-
mation about a
function key. After
initiating Help, you
can retrieve infor-
mation about a
particular function
key by pressing it.
In this example,
the [F2] (Search)
key was pressed.

```
Search

     Searches forward (F2) or backward (Shift-F2) through your text for a
     specific combination of characters and/or codes.  After entering the
     search text, press Search again to start the search.  If the text is
     found, the cursor will be positioned just after (to the right of) it.
     Lowercase letters in the search text match both lowercase and uppercase.
     Uppercase letters match only uppercase.

     Extended Search
     Pressing Home before pressing Search extends the search into headers,
     footers, footnotes, endnotes, graphics box captions, and text boxes.  To
     continue the extended search, press Home, Search.




Selection: 0                                (Press ENTER to exit Help)
```

Figure 1.9

After iniating Help, you can retrieve information about a particular topic by typing the first character of the topic. In this example, the letter M was pressed.

```
Features [M]                        WordPerfect Key   Keystrokes

Macro Editor                        Macro Define      Ctrl-F10
Macro Commands                      Macro Commands    Ctrl-PgUp
Macro Commands, Help On             Macro Define      Ctrl-F10
Macros, Define                      Macro Define      Ctrl-F10
Macros, Execute                     Macro             Alt-F10
Macros, Keyboard Definition         Setup             Shft-F1,5
Mail Merge                          Merge/Sort        Ctrl-F9,1
Main Dictionary Location            Setup             Shft-F1,6,3
Manual Hyphenation                  Format            Shft-F8,1,1
Map, Keyboard                       Setup             Shft-F1,5,8
Map Special Characters              Setup             Shft-F1,5
Margin Release                      Margin Release    Shft-Tab
Margins - Left and Right            Format            Shft-F8,1,7
Margins - Top and Bottom            Format            Shft-F8,2,5
Mark Text For Index (Block On)      Mark Text         Alt-F5,3
Mark Text For List (Block On)       Mark Text         Alt-F5,2
Mark Text For ToA (Block On)        Mark Text         Alt-F5,4
Mark Text For ToC (Block On)        Mark Text         Alt-F5,1
Master Document                     Mark Text         Alt-F5,2
Math                                Columns/Table     Alt-F7,3
More... Press m to continue.

Selection: 0                                      (Press ENTER to exit Help)
```

Quick Reference
Help F3

Used to obtain information about a particular function key or about how to execute a particular command.
1. To initiate the HELP command, press F3.
2. Next, press a function key or a letter that corresponds to a command.
3. To exit the HELP command, press Enter or the Space Bar.

CREATING A DOCUMENT

Your cursor should still be blinking in the upper left-hand corner of your screen. This marks where the first character you type will appear. WordPerfect operates in **Insert mode.** Therefore anything you type right now—numbers, letters, and other characters—will be inserted at the current cursor location. In addition, pressing the Space Bar inserts spaces and pressing Enter inserts blank lines. The only keys you can use to move the cursor within a document without affecting the text are the cursor-movement keys.

We will now lead you through typing the paragraph pictured in Figure 1.10.

Figure 1.10

Practice
paragraph

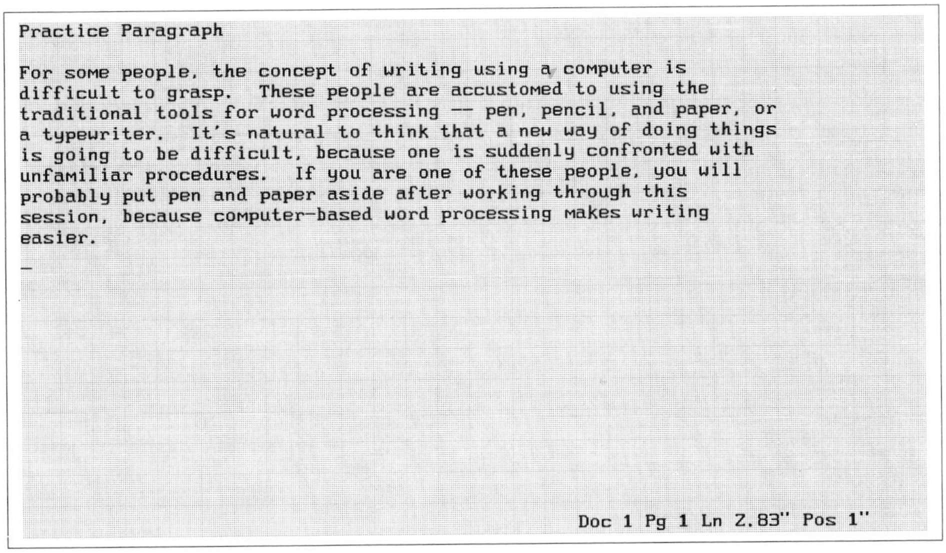

```
Practice Paragraph

For some people, the concept of writing using a computer is
difficult to grasp.  These people are accustomed to using the
traditional tools for word processing -- pen, pencil, and paper, or
a typewriter.  It's natural to think that a new way of doing things
is going to be difficult, because one is suddenly confronted with
unfamiliar procedures.  If you are one of these people, you will
probably put pen and paper aside after working through this
session, because computer-based word processing makes writing
easier.
_




                                                   Doc 1 Pg 1 Ln 2.83" Pos 1"
```

INSERTING TEXT: INSERT VERSUS TYPEOVER

To illustrate the fundamentals of inserting text, this section leads you through editing the words "Practice Paragraph."

1. The first item of information you will type is the word "Paragraph." You will insert the word "Practice" shortly.
    TYPE: Paragraph

2. The cursor should be positioned one character to the right of the word "Paragraph."
    PRESS: ⬅ *to move the cursor to the left nine times*

3. The cursor should be positioned beneath the "P" of "Paragraph."
    TYPE: Practice
    PRESS: Space Bar

4. Note that the word "Practice" (followed by a space) was inserted before the word "Paragraph." If you don't want to operate in insert mode, you can press (Insert) and WordPerfect will go into **Typeover mode** (most WordPerfect users stay in Insert mode 90% of the time). To illustrate Typeover mode:
    PRESS: ⬅ *to position the cursor beneath the "P" of "Practice"*
    PRESS: (Insert)
    The text "Typeover" should be displaying in the bottom-left corner.
    TYPE: My
    The screen should look similar to Figure 1.11.

Figure 1.11

Insert mode
versus Type-
over mode.
WordPerfect
operates in
Insert mode.
Pressing
[Insert] takes
WordPerfect
into Typeover
mode. In this
mode, what
you type over-
strikes char-
acters in your
document.

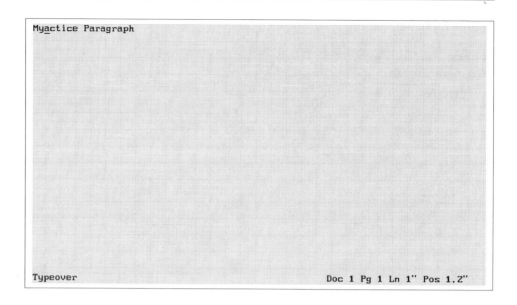

The word "My" should have overwritten the first two characters of "Practice."

5. To insert a space and "Pr" in the correct position:
   PRESS: [Insert]
   WordPerfect is back in Insert mode.
   PRESS: Space Bar
   TYPE: Pr
   The screen should look like Figure 1.12.

Figure 1.12

Inserting char-
acters in your
document

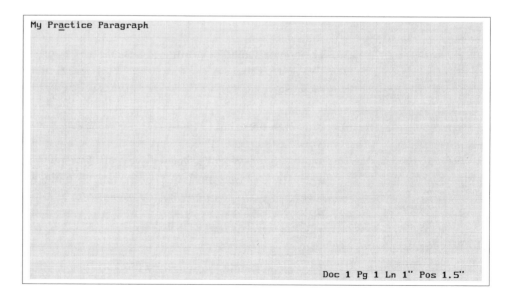

6. When (Enter) is pressed, blank lines are inserted in your document. To illustrate:
   PRESS: *the cursor-movement keys to position the cursor beneath the letter "P" of "Paragraph"*
   PRESS: (Enter) *four times*
   The word "Paragraph" was brought down *with* the cursor, and blank lines were inserted. In the next section you learn how to get the word "Paragraph" back to its original position.

....

Quick Reference
Inserting Text

Insert text, spaces, or blank lines using the arrow keys to position the cursor where you want the new items to appear and then either typing in the text (for inserted text), pressing the Space Bar or (Tab) (for inserted spaces), or pressing (Enter) (for blank lines).

....

DELETING TEXT: (Delete) VERSUS (BackSpace)

The two keys commonly used to delete text are (Delete) and (BackSpace). Whereas (Delete) deletes the character the cursor is positioned on, (BackSpace) deletes the character to the left of the cursor.

1. To get the word "Paragraph" back to its original position using (Delete):
   PRESS: *the cursor-movement keys to move the cursor to where the "P" of "Paragraph" was positioned originally (Figure 1.13). (In this case, you will need to press (↑) three times and (←) once. Pressing (←) moved the cursor to the end of the previous line.)*

Figure 1.13

The cursor is now in the appropriate position; by pressing (Delete) four times, you will move the word "Para-graph" to the current cursor position.

```
My Practice _


Paragraph




                                              Doc 1 Pg 1 Ln 1" Pos 2.2"
```

2. The cursor should be positioned where "Paragraph" was originally positioned. Do the following to move "Paragraph" back to its original position.
    PRESS: (Delete) *four times*
    "Paragraph" should have moved back to its original position.

3. To illustrate the use of (BackSpace):
    PRESS: *the cursor-movement keys until the cursor is positioned beneath the "P" of "Practice"*
    PRESS: (BackSpace) *three times*
    The word "My" and the following space have now been deleted.

4. To move the cursor down two lines without moving "Paragraph" down also, you must move the cursor to the end of the current line.
    PRESS: (→) *so that the cursor is positioned one character to the right of "Paragraph"*
    PRESS: (Enter) *twice*
    The cursor should have moved down two lines, and "Paragraph" should have stayed in its original position. The cursor is now in the appropriate position for you to begin typing the practice paragraph.

Quick Reference
Deleting Text:
(Delete) *vs.*
(BackSpace)

1. Delete text, spaces, or blank lines using the arrow keys to position the cursor on the text, space or blank line that you want to delete and then pressing (Delete) until the item you're deleting is gone.
2. Use (BackSpace) to delete text or spaces to the left of the cursor.

Table 1.1 lists a few additional methods for deleting text in a document.

Table 1.1	(Delete)	Deletes the character the cursor is positioned on
Methods for Deleting Text	(BackSpace)	Deletes the character to the left of the cursor
	(Ctrl)+(BackSpace)	Deletes the word the cursor is positioned on
	(Ctrl)+(End)	Deletes to the end of the current line
	(Ctrl)+(PgDn)	Deletes to the end of the page

WORD WRAP

When typing the practice paragraph, you will press (Enter) only once—that is, at the end of the paragraph. *Don't press* (Enter) *at the end of every line.* The words you type will automatically wrap around to the next line when WordPerfect reaches the right margin.

> TYPE: For some people, the concept of writing using a computer is difficult to grasp. These people are accustomed to using the traditional tools for word processing -- pen, pencil, and paper, or a typewriter. It's natural to think that a new way of doing things is going to be difficult, because one is suddenly confronted with unfamiliar procedures. If you are one of these people, you will probably put pen and paper aside after working through this session, because computer-based word processing makes writing easier.
> PRESS: (Enter)
> The screen should now look like Figure 1.10.

Quick Reference   When typing a paragraph, don't press (Enter) at the end of every line. Only
Word Wrap   press (Enter) at the end of the paragraph.

SAVING YOUR WORK

For now, your document is stored in RAM. RAM is always empty after the electricity to your computer is cut off. So, if someone accidentally trips on the power cord connected to your computer right now and pulls it out, you lose your document. When working with applications software, you should periodically save your work onto a permanent nonvolatile storage device such as a diskette or a hard disk.

SAVING A DOCUMENT ((F10))

To save your work, use the **Save key** ((F10)). *Using the menu bar, choose Save from the File menu.* You will save this document as WPDOC1 onto the Advantage Diskette.

Perform the following steps:

1. Make sure that your Advantage Diskette is in drive A: of your computer.

2. It doesn't matter where the cursor is positioned, so you can proceed with the SAVE command.
    PRESS: (F10)

3. The text "Document to be saved:" should appear on the bottom left of the screen. WordPerfect is waiting for you to tell it where you want to save this document (A:) and what you want to name it (WPDOC1). To save the document onto the diskette in drive A: (it doesn't matter whether you use upper- or lowercase letters):
    TYPE: A:WPDOC1
    PRESS: (Enter)

The WPDOC1 document has now been saved onto the Advantage Diskette.

Quick Reference   1. PRESS: (F10)
Save (F10)   2. Key in the disk drive designation followed by a filename (for example, B:FILENAME)
                             3. PRESS: (Enter)

SAVING A DOCUMENT MORE THAN ONCE ((F10))

What if you make some new changes to the current document (the one you just saved)? You should save your work again so that the updated document in RAM will replace the older version of the document on the disk.

1. Pretend you have made some changes to the WPDOC1 document.
    PRESS: (F10)

2. The correct disk drive (A: or B:) and filename (WPDOC1) should automatically appear after the text "Document to be Saved:".
    PRESS: (Enter)

3. The message "Replace WPDOC1? (Y/N)" should appear. WordPerfect is asking if you want to replace the old, or last saved, version of your document on disk with the updated contents of RAM. Since you do want to update the document stored on disk:
    CHOOSE: Yes

Again, because your documents are stored in RAM (volatile storage) while you're creating them, you should save your work periodically onto either a diskette or a hard disk (nonvolatile storage).

Quick Reference
Saving a Document
More Than Once:
F10

1. PRESS: F10
2. The correct disk drive designation and filename should automatically display.
3. PRESS: Enter
4. To replace the contents on disk with the updated contents of RAM: CHOOSE: Yes

---

BEGINNING A NEW DOCUMENT (F7)

The procedure to begin work on a new or different document uses the **Exit key** (F7). *Using the menu bar, choose Exit from the File menu.* Because it is likely you will want, at some point, to begin work on a new document, we will show you the procedure now. We will then walk you through retrieving WPDOC1 from the Advantage Diskette.

1. PRESS: F7
   When WordPerfect asks whether you want to save your document:
   CHOOSE: No
   (Note: You typed N because you had already saved your document. However, if you hadn't yet saved your work, you could have saved it at this point by typing Y, the name of the document, and pressing Enter.)

2. When WordPerfect asks if you want to exit WordPerfect:
   CHOOSE: No

You pressed N because you are not exiting WordPerfect entirely; you are only clearing one document from RAM in order to begin a new one. The screen should now be cleared of your document and look like it did after you first loaded WordPerfect.

Quick Reference
Clearing RAM After
Using the SAVE
Command: F7

1. To initiate the EXIT command:
   PRESS: F7
2. CHOOSE: No, No

RETRIEVING YOUR FILES

To work with a file that has been previously saved onto the disk, you must retrieve it into RAM. Remember that WordPerfect always inserts the retrieved document at the current cursor position. Therefore, if your cursor is in the middle of a document, the retrieved document will be inserted at the cursor position. If you don't want the document inserted at the current cursor position, you should first save your work and then clear the screen using the EXIT (F7) command. In the next two sections we describe two methods for retrieving a file.

RETRIEVING A DOCUMENT: YOU KNOW THE FILENAME (Shift+F10)

Retrieving a document when you know the filename can be accomplished by using the **Retrieve** key combination (Shift+F10). *Using the menu bar, choose Retrieve from the File menu.* To retrieve the document called WPDOC1 from the Advantage Diskette, perform the following procedure:

1. To initiate the RETRIEVE command:
    PRESS: Shift+F10

2. WordPerfect is waiting for you to specify the disk drive designation and filename of the file you want to retrieve:
    TYPE: A:WPDOC1
    PRESS: Enter

The document named WPDOC1 should be displaying on the screen.

CAUTION: If you retrieve a document without clearing RAM first (F7, No, No), WordPerfect will ask if you want to retrieve the document into the current document. If this isn't your intention, choose No, save your work, clear RAM, and then retrieve the new document.

Quick Reference
Retrieve
Shift+F10

1. PRESS: Shift+F10
2. Key in the disk drive designation and the name of the file you want to retrieve (for example, A:FILENAME)
3. PRESS: Enter

RETRIEVING A DOCUMENT: YOU'VE FORGOTTEN THE FILENAME ([F5])

Unfortunately, it's very easy to forget what names you have given to stored files—especially if you are working with a large number of files. The **List Files key** ([F5]) provides a means of retrieving a file if you have forgotten its name because it will list the names of the files stored on a disk. *Using the menu bar, choose List Files from the File menu.*

1. PRESS: [F5]

2. To list the files stored on the Advantage Diskette in drive A:
    TYPE: A:
    PRESS: [Enter]

3. A list of the files stored on the diskette in drive A: should be displaying on the screen. The screen should look similar to Figure 1.14. Note that one of the options on the bottom of the screen is "Retrieve." At this point you could highlight the file you want to retrieve and then choose the Retrieve option. Because you retrieved the WPDOC1 file in the last section, you don't need to retrieve the file again. To exit to the typing area, press the Cancel key ([F1]). WPDOC1 should be on the screen again.

Figure 1.14

The List Files menu

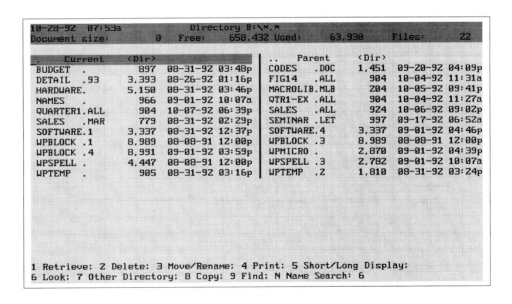

....

Quick Reference

List Files F5 *:*
Retrieving a File

1. PRESS: F5
2. Type in the disk drive designation of the disk with the stored files (for example, A:).
3. PRESS: Enter
4. Use the cursor-movement keys to highlight the file you want to retrieve.
5. CHOOSE: Retrieve

....

CURSOR-MOVEMENT COMMANDS

Especially when documents are longer than a page, you can save time if you know how to efficiently move the cursor around a document. Until now, you've been using the ↑, ↓, ←, and → cursor-movement keys to move the cursor, but, as shown in Table 1.2, other methods exist. In this section, you will use the WPBLOCK.1 file stored on the Advantage Diskette to practice using these other methods for moving the cursor.

Table 1.2

Cursor-Movement
Methods

Horizontal Movement	Keys
Character left or right	← or →
Word right	Ctrl + →
Word left	Ctrl + ←
Right edge of screen	Home + →
Left edge of screen	Home + ←

Vertical Movement	Keys
Line up or down	↑ or ↓
Top of screen	Home, ↑
Bottom of screen	Home, ↓
Top of current page	Ctrl + Home, ↑
End of current page	Ctrl + Home, ↓
Top of previous page	PgUp
Top of next page	PgDn
Beginning of document	Home, Home, ↑
End of document	Home, Home, ↓
Go To page #	Ctrl + Home, press #, Enter
# Lines up	Esc, press #, ↑
# Lines down	Esc, press #, ↓

Perform the following steps:

1. To clear RAM so you can work on a different document:
    PRESS: [F7]
    CHOOSE: <u>N</u>o, <u>N</u>o

2. Retrieve a copy of the file named WPBLOCK.1 from the Advantage Diskette using the following procedure:
    PRESS: [Shift]+[F10]
    TYPE: A:WPBLOCK.1
    PRESS: [Enter]

3. To move the cursor to the top of page 2:
    PRESS: [PgDn]
    You can tell what page the cursor is on by looking at the status line.

4. To move the cursor to the top of page 3:
    PRESS: [PgDn]

5. To move the cursor to the bottom of the document:
    PRESS: [Home], [Home]
    PRESS: [↓]

6. To move the cursor to the top of the document:
    PRESS: [Home], [Home]
    PRESS: [↑]

7. To move the cursor to a specific page, such as page 4:
    PRESS: [Ctrl]+[Home]
    TYPE: 4
    PRESS: [Enter]
    This procedure is especially useful when working with long documents, because it allows you to skip many pages at a time.

8. To position the cursor on the first line of the first paragraph on page 4:
    PRESS: [↓]

9. To move the cursor to the end of the line:
    PRESS: [End]

10. To move the cursor to the beginning of the line:
    PRESS: [Home]
    PRESS: [←]

11. To move the cursor to the right, one word at a time, hold [Ctrl] down and press [→]:
    PRESS: [Ctrl]+[→]

12. To move the cursor to the left, one word at a time, hold `Ctrl` down and press `←`:
    PRESS: `Ctrl`+`←`
    Practice on your own some of the cursor-movement commands listed in Table 1.2.

13. To clear RAM of this document:
    PRESS: `F7`
    CHOOSE: No, No

EDITING A DOCUMENT

In this section you retrieve WPDOC1 (you created this earlier in this session) and then edit it so that it looks like the document pictured in Figure 1.15. You will perform the following editing tasks:

Figure 1.15

The edited
WPDOC1
document

```
My Practice Paragraph

For some people, the concept of writing using a computer is
difficult to grasp.  These people are accustomed to using the
traditional tools for word processing -- pen, pencil, and paper, or
a typewriter.
    It's natural to think that a new way of doing things is going
to be difficult, because one is suddenly confronted with unfamiliar
procedures.  But word processing software offers users so many
advantages that even if you are one of these people, you will
probably put pen and paper aside after working through this
session.  The following includes a partial list of what you can do
with word processing software to edit a document.
    1.   Center text between the margins
    2.   Insert and delete text
    3.   Change a document from single- to double-spacing
_



C:\IRWIN\DISKETTE\WPDOC1                        Doc 1 Pg 1 Ln 3.67" Pos 1"
```

1. Break the paragraph into two paragraphs.

2. Insert and delete text.

3. Add text to the bottom of the document.

BREAKING ONE PARAGRAPH INTO TWO

Because WordPerfect operates in Insert mode, if you press the (Enter) key on a line that contains text, the text will move down to the next line. This procedure can be used to break one paragraph into two.

1. To retrieve WPDOC1:
    PRESS: (Shift)+(F10)
    TYPE: A:WPDOC1
    PRESS: (Enter)

2. Position the cursor beneath the "I" of "It's" at the beginning of the third sentence.

3. PRESS: (Enter)
    PRESS: (Tab)
    ((Tab) moves the cursor to the right five spaces.)

INSERTING TEXT AND DELETING TEXT

Perform the following steps:

1. Position the cursor at the beginning of the second sentence in the second paragraph (beneath the "I" of "If ").

2. TYPE: But word processing software offers users so many advantages that even if

3. To delete the second "If ":
    PRESS: (Delete) *twice*

4. To end the sentence after the word "session":
    a. Position the cursor on the comma that follows the word "session"
    b. PRESS: (Delete) *once*
    c. TYPE: .

5. To delete the rest of the sentence:
    a. Position the cursor beneath the "b" of "because."
    b. PRESS: (Delete) *until the rest of the sentence has been deleted*

ADDING TEXT TO THE BOTTOM OF THE DOCUMENT

Perform the following steps to add text to this document.

1. The cursor should be positioned two spaces to the right of the word "session."
   TYPE: The following includes a partial list of what you can do with word processing software to edit a document:
   PRESS: [Enter]

2. PRESS: [Tab]
   TYPE: 1.
   PRESS: [Tab]
   TYPE: Center text between the margins
   PRESS: [Enter]

3. PRESS: [Tab]
   TYPE: 2.
   PRESS: [Tab]
   TYPE: Insert and delete text
   PRESS: [Enter]

4. PRESS: [Tab]
   TYPE: 3.
   PRESS: [Tab]
   TYPE: Change a document from single- to double-spacing
   PRESS: [Enter]
   Your document should look like Figure 1.15.

REVEALING CODES ([Alt]+[F3]) OR ([F11])

When you type characters such as the letters A through Z, they appear on the screen. However, WordPerfect embeds some "invisible" characters, or codes, into the document as you're working on it. Revealing these invisible codes can be quite helpful, especially after you've pressed a few keys accidentally and discover that some of your editing functions don't work because you inadvertently inserted an unwanted code. Once the embedded codes are revealed, you can delete an unwanted code by positioning the cursor on it and pressing [Delete]. The **REVEAL CODES** command can be accessed by holding [Alt] down and pressing [F3], or by pressing only [F11], if you have one on your keyboard. *Using the menu bar, choose Reveal Codes from the Edit menu.*

To see what codes WordPerfect has embedded in the WPDOC2 document, do the following:

1. Position the cursor at the top of the document.

2. PRESS: [Alt]+[F3] (*or* [F11])

3. The screen should look like Figure 1.16. Many people find this display confusing. The top half of the screen displays the document without the embedded codes, and the bottom half of the screen displays the document with the embedded codes revealed. When the cursor is moved through the document, it is simultaneously moved through both the top and bottom document screens. The SRt (soft return) codes at the end of many of the lines are WordPerfect's way of symbolizing word wrap. The HRt (hard return) code at the end of each paragraph means [Enter] was pressed. Table 1.3 includes a partial list of the codes that WordPerfect embeds in your documents.

Figure 1.16

Revealing codes. Document codes can be revealed by pressing [Alt]+[F3].

```
My Practice Paragraph

For some people, the concept of writing using a computer is
difficult to grasp.  These people are accustomed to using the
traditional tools for word processing -- pen, pencil, and paper, or
a typewriter.
     It's natural to think that a new way of doing things is going
to be difficult, because one is suddenly confronted with unfamiliar
procedures.  But word processing software offers users so many
advantages that even if you are one of these people, you will
probably put pen and paper aside after working through this
C:\IRWIN\DISKETTE\WPDOC1                         Doc 1 Pg 1 Ln 1" Pos 1"
```
```
My Practice Paragraph[HRt]
[HRt]
For some people, the concept of writing using a computer is[SRt]
difficult to grasp.  These people are accustomed to using the[SRt]
traditional tools for word processing [-][-] pen, pencil, and paper, or[SRt]
a typewriter.  [HRt]
[Tab]It's natural to think that a new way of doing things is going[SRt]
to be difficult, because one is suddenly confronted with unfamiliar[SRt]
procedures.  But word processing software offers users so many[SRt]
advantages that even if you are one of these people, you will[SRt]

Press Reveal Codes to restore screen
```

4. To turn the Reveal Codes option off:
   PRESS: [Alt]+[F3] (*or* [F11])

Quick Reference
Reveal Codes

1. PRESS: [Alt]+[F3] (*or* [F11])
2. To return to your document:
   PRESS: [Alt]+[F3] (*or* [F11])

Table 1.3	Code	Description
Partial List of Embedded Codes	[Flsh Rt]	Flush right
	[BOLD] [bold]	Begin and end boldfacing
	[Center]	Centering
	[Header N:type;text]	Header definition
	[Footer N:type;text]	Footer definition
	[HPg]	Hard page break inserted by the user
	[HRt]	Hard return inserted by pressing Enter
	[~RA Indent]	Beginning of left indent
	[~RA Indent ~LA]	Beginning of left and right indent
	[L/R Mar:n,n]	Left and right margin settings
	[Pg Num:n]	Page number set to n
	[Pg Numbering: position]	Position of page number
	[SPg]	Soft page break
	[SRt]	Soft return (word wrap)
	[TAB]	Tab
	[UND] [und]	Begin and end underlining

SAVING THE REVISED DOCUMENT UNDER A DIFFERENT NAME

In this section, you will save the revised document in RAM onto the Advantage Diskette. However, you will give the revised document the name of WPDOC2.

1. As we mentioned earlier, when you save a document using WordPerfect, it doesn't matter where the cursor is positioned.
    PRESS: F10

2. The text "Document to be Saved:" should appear on the bottom left of the screen. WordPerfect is waiting for you to tell it where you want to save this document and what you want to name it. To save the document onto the Advantage Diskette in drive A: with a new filename:
    TYPE: A:WPDOC2
    PRESS: Enter

The document has now been saved onto the Advantage Diskette under the name WPDOC2.

PRINTING A DOCUMENT (Shift+F7)

To print a document, use the **Print** key combination (Shift+F7). *Using the menu bar, choose Print from the File menu.* When you print a document, WordPerfect makes many different assumptions (default values) about what the printed output will look like, including (1) the width of the margins and (2) whether the right margin will appear lined up (even-justified) or jagged (left-justified). Because these assumptions are based on how most users want their documents formatted, you will probably find that, more often than not, WordPerfect's default values are fine for your purposes. However, by using WordPerfect's Format menu (Shift+F8), you can change any default printing assumptions (we lead you through using the Format menu and changing WordPerfect's printing assumptions in Session 4). In the following steps we lead you through printing the document without changing any of WordPerfect's default values.

1. PRESS: Shift+F7
    The screen should look similar to Figure 1.17.

Figure 1.17

The WordPerfect Print menu

```
Print

    1 - Full Document
    2 - Page
    3 - Document on Disk
    4 - Control Printer
    5 - Multiple Pages
    6 - View Document
    7 - Initialize Printer


Options

    S - Select Printer                    HP LaserJet Series II
    B - Binding Offset                    0"
    N - Number of Copies                  1
    U - Multiple Copies Generated by      WordPerfect
    G - Graphics Quality                  Medium
    T - Text Quality                      High




Selection: 0
```

2. To print the entire document:
    CHOOSE: Full Document

Quick Reference
Print (**Shift**)+(**F7**)

1. PRESS: (Shift)+(F7)
2. To print the entire document:
    CHOOSE: <u>F</u>ull Document

EXITING WORDPERFECT

Remember to save your work before exiting WordPerfect; otherwise you will lose the latest changes you've made to your document. Because saving is such an important step before exiting, the EXIT command also provides you with the opportunity to save your work (Save Document Y/N?). If you have already saved your work, you can respond by typing N to the save prompt.

To exit WordPerfect, the following steps must be used:

1. PRESS: (F7)

2. Respond to the save prompt by choosing either <u>Y</u>es to save your work or <u>N</u>o if you have already saved your work. If you choose to save your work, follow the screen prompts until you are prompted to exit WordPerfect.

3. When prompted to exit WordPerfect:
    CHOOSE: <u>Y</u>es

CAUTION: If you don't exit WordPerfect before turning the computer off, you will leave a number of files "open" on the disk. The next time you load WordPerfect, the following message will be displayed on the screen: `Are there any other versions of WordPerfect running on this machine?` After the prompt, type N.

SUMMARY

This session introduced you to working with word processing software programs, specifically WordPerfect 5.1. We began the session exploring the advantages of word processing using microcomputers. Then, after loading WordPerfect, we described the WordPerfect screen and how to access Help information using (F3).

In the latter half of the session, you created a practice document and practiced using Insert and Typeover modes. You also learned how to remove characters using Delete and BackSpace. Once you created the document you used F10 to save it onto the Advantage Diskette, Shift+F10 to retrieve it, and then Shift+F7 to print.

The REVEAL CODES command (Alt+F3) enables you to see the codes that WordPerfect embeds in your documents. Revealing these invisible codes can be quite helpful, especially after you've pressed a few keys accidentally and discover that some of your editing functions don't work because you inadvertently inserted an unwanted code. (In subsequent sessions, you will reveal codes after issuing formatting commands.) You can delete unwanted codes using Delete or Backspace.

COMMAND SUMMARY

The following table provides a list of the commands and procedures covered in this session.

Table 1.4	F1	Cancel the current command or restore deleted text
Command Summary	F3	Obtain Help information
	F10, type disk drive and filename, Enter	Save a file
	F7, No, No	Begin a new document
	Shift+F10, type disk drive and filename, Enter	Retrieve a document when you know the filename
	F5, Enter, highlight filename, Retrieve	Retrieve a document when you've forgotten the filename
	Alt+F3	Reveal codes
	Shift+F7, Full document	Print a document
	F7, No, Yes	Exit WordPerfect

KEY TERMS

block operation   By using block operations, it is possible to move, delete, copy, and format entire sentences, paragraphs, and pages by issuing commands.

Cancel key (F1)   In WordPerfect, if a menu is displaying on the screen, this key enables the user to cancel out of a menu; if a document is displaying on the screen, this key enables the user to restore deleted text to the document.

cursor   Indicator on video display screen that shows where next character or space that is entered will appear.

character formatting commands   A type of **formatting command** that enables you to improve the appearance of your document using underlining, boldfacing, centering, and other commands.

document cycle   The stages of creating a document, using word processing software for entering, editing, spell-checking, formatting, saving and retrieving, and printing. The cycle may also include merging text from separate documents into a single document.

document formatting commands   A type of **formatting command** that enables you to improve the appearance of your document using commands to change margins, paper size, and include headers and footers in a document.

editing   Process of changing text—for example, inserting and deleting.

Exit key (F7)   In WordPerfect, this key is used to exit menus and WordPerfect. (Before exiting WordPerfect, you are prompted to save your work.)

footer   Descriptive information (such as page number and date) that appears at the bottom of each page of a document.

formatting commands   These commands enable you to improve the appearance of your documents.

header   Descriptive information (such as page number and date) that appears at the top of each page of a document.

Help key (F3)   In WordPerfect, this key is used to obtain Help information about the current command, a particular function key, or a particular topic.

Insert mode   In **word processing**, the editing mode that allows the user to insert text at the position of the cursor without typing over existing text. Compare **Typeover mode**.

List Files key (F5)   In WordPerfect, this key is used to list on the screen the files stored on the current disk; also used to erase, rename, copy, and print files.

merging   Bringing together information from two different files.

page formatting commands   A type of **formatting command** that enables you to improve the appearance of your document; for example, hard page breaks, line spacing commands, tab changes, and indent commands.

Print (Shift+F7)   In WordPerfect, this command is used to print documents out on the printer.

Retrieve (Shift+F10)   WordPerfect command that enables the user to retrieve into RAM a copy of a file that is stored on disk.

Reveal Codes (Alt+F3) (F11)   Enables the user to display all the codes that WordPerfect has included (embedded) in a document.

Save key (F10)   Enables the user to save work in WordPerfect; after pressing this key, the user must supply a name for the file being saved.

scrolling   Activity of moving text up or down on the video display screen.

search and replace   In **word processing**, the activity of automatically searching for and replacing text in a document.

spelling checker   In **word processing**, programs that check a document for spelling errors.

system requirements   Refers to the hardware and software that is required to use a particular software application.

thesaurus   Lists of words that have similar meaning to a given word.

Typeover mode   In **word processing**, the mode of inserting text in which existing text is typed over as new text is typed in. Compare **Insert mode**.

word processing software   Program enabling user to create and edit documents by inserting, deleting, and moving text. Some programs also offer formatting features such as variable margins and different type sizes and styles, as well as more advanced features that border on desktop publishing.

word wrap   In word processing, when the cursor reaches the right-hand margin of a line it automatically returns (wraps around) to the left-hand margin of the line below and continues the text; the user does not have to hit a key to make the cursor move down to the next line.

EXERCISES

SHORT ANSWER

1. Why is the REVEAL CODES (Alt+F3) command important?
2. What does the term *merging* refer to?
3. What is the document cycle?
4. Why is it significant to know that WordPerfect operates in Insert mode?

5. When you are using WordPerfect, why is it important to clear RAM before retrieving another file?
6. What happens if you press (Enter) when the cursor is in the middle of a paragraph?
7. What are headers and footers used for?
8. What is meant by the term *word wrap*?
9. What is a block operation?
10 What is the function of the Cancel ((F1)) key?

HANDS-ON

1. In this exercise, you will practice using the HELP key to perform the following tasks and answer the following questions:
   a. PRESS: (F3)
   b. Display the WordPerfect template.
   c. What keys must you press to change the justification of a document?
   d. What keys must you press to change the current tab settings?
   e. What does (F4) do for you?
   f. Exit the HELP command back to the document screen.

2. Type in the following text and then save it onto the Advantage Diskette as BACKUP.DOC. Print BACKUP.DOC.

```
Backing Up Your Microcomputer System
by: your name

The scenario: You've stored a year's worth of
client information on your hard disk. You are able
to retrieve client information easily onto the
screen. You have confidence in your computer
system until the hard disk crashes; the read/write
heads fall onto the surface of the disk making the
disk unusable and causing the loss of all the data
stored on the disk! Well, at least you have a
backup copy of your client files. What? You don't?
   One of the most important tasks involved in
maintaining a microcomputer system is to make
copies of--or a backup of--your data files. A
popular rule of thumb is to never let more time
pass between backups than the amount of data
represented that you are willing to lose in a disk
disaster. Depending on the amount of activity on a
system, hard disks should be backed up at the end
of each day or each week. All managers should make
sure that office policies include backup
procedures.
```

3. To practice cursor-movement commands, retrieve HARDWARE and then perform the following steps:
   a. Move the cursor to the bottom of the document.
   b. Move the cursor to the top of the document.
   c. Move the cursor to the end of the current line.
   d. Move the cursor one word to the right.
   e. Move the cursor to the top of the next page.
   f. Clear the screen without saving this document.

4. Create the document pictured below. Make sure you include the current date at the beginning of the letter and your name and job position (real or made up) at the end of the letter. Save this document onto the Advantage Diskette as WPLETTER.

```
current date




Mr. Andrew San Martino
210 Spruce Way
San Jose, CA 94063

Dear Mr. San Martino:

I received your letter the other day regarding the
upcoming event. I am in total agreement with you
about limiting the number of persons who can
attend to 150. In addition, your idea of having
the event catered sounds great.

And now to move onto a different subject. I
noticed that the letter you wrote me was typed
using a typewriter. You sure do use correction
fluid well! Or I should say, you sure do use quite
a bit of it! Just teasing ... but with the number
of letters you write, you really should think of
purchasing a microcomputer and word processing
software. I am sure you will save time.

If you are interested, you should come over to my
office and I will show you some of the
fundamentals that relate to word processing. We
could even use my word processing software to
design and print all of the invitations to the
upcoming event!

With best regards,


your name
your job position
```

a. Print WPLETTER.

b. Insert the following text between the second and third paragraphs:

```
Specifically, word processing software makes it
much easier to make changes to a document by
allowing you to:

1. Insert text
2. Move text
3. Copy text
4. Delete text
5. Perform block operations
6. Spell-check
7. Include special format enhancements such as
boldfacing, underlining, and centering
```

c. Save this updated document as WPLETTER (it will need to replace the first version of WPLETTER). Print WPLETTER again.

5. Create the following document (make sure to include your name in the closing of the letter) and then save the document onto the Advantage Diskette as ABCLTR:

```
June 28, 1993



Mr. S. Luis Obispo
Manager, Sales
ABC Realty Inc.
1399 Primrose Lane
Albany, GA 31705

Dear Luis:

Per our discussion yesterday, please accept this
letter as confirmation on your order for computer
equipment, deliverable next week.

We apologize for the delay in getting the hardware
you requested. All equipment has now arrived and
is presently being configured.

As ordered, five computers will be installed: one
at Reception, two for sales, one for accounting,
and the last one for yourself. We will also be
installing DOS 3.3, Windows 3.0, and Word for
Windows 2.0 at that time.

Training on these software programs will begin the
week after installation, per the schedule arranged
```

in our meeting. The cost of the training is
included in the total cost of the equipment.

If I can be of any further assistance before the
installation or if you have any questions, please
do not hesitate to contact me.

Yours sincerely,
Tick Talk Technology

your name
Accounts Representative

a. In the third paragraph, perform the following editing changes:

Text Before Editing	Text After Editing
DOS 3.3	Microsoft DOS 5.0
Windows 3.0	Microsoft Windows 3.1
at that time	the next morning

b. Remove the entire fourth paragraph, starting with "Training on...".
c. Enter the phone number (800)999-9999 below the last line.
d. Save the document as ABCLTR.
e. Clear the document from your screen.
f. Retrieve ABCLTR from the Advantage Diskette.
g. Edit the phone number to read (800)000-0000.
h. Save and print ABCLTR and then clear it from your screen.

6. Clear the RAM of your computer so that you're not viewing a document. Retrieve SOFTWARE.1 from the Advantage Diskette. Perform the following tasks:
a. Insert three blank lines at the top of this document. Type CATEGORIES OF APPLICATIONS SOFTWARE on the first line and your name on the second line.
b. Review the letter for spelling or grammatical errors by moving the cursor through the document. Edit the document to correct any errors.
c. Delete the third sentence in the first paragraph.
d. Insert the following sentence after the first sentence in the fourth paragraph: (Software is available for almost any hobby you can think of!)
e. Save (and replace) this document onto the Advantage Diskette as SOFTWARE.1.
f. Print SOFTWARE.1.

7. Write a one-page document describing some of the useful features of word processing software. Include your name and the current date at the top of the document. Save this letter onto your Advantage Diskette as FEATURES, and then print the document.

SESSION 2

FORMATTING COMMANDS

In this session you learn how to customize your documents to meet your particular needs. To accomplish this, you will issue formatting commands that will change some of the assumptions made by WordPerfect about how your documents will appear on the screen and when printed.

PREVIEW

When you have completed this session, you will be able to:

Use character formatting commands.
·
Indent paragraphs.
·
Change line spacing.
·
Change tab settings.
·
Force a page break.

Why Is This Session Important?
Character Formatting Commands
    Flush Right (`Alt`+`F6`) and Date
       (`Shift`+`F5`)
    Center (`Shift`+`F6`)
    Underline (`F8`) and Bold (`F6`)
    Combining Commands
Character Formatting Using Block Commands
    Highlighting Blocks
    Underlining (`F8`) and Boldfacing (`F6`) a
       Block
    Uppercase/Lowercase (`Alt`+`F4`,
       `Shift`+`F3`)
Indenting
Changing Line Spacing (`Shift`+`F8`)
Changing Tab Settings (`Shift`+`F8`)
Forcing a Page Break (`Ctrl`+`Enter`)
Summary
    Command Summary
Key Terms
Exercises
    Short Answer
    Hands-On

WHY IS THIS SESSION IMPORTANT?

In this session you will learn how to enhance documents to meet your needs or the needs of a particular business task. First you will use formatting commands to change the way characters appear in your documents. Specifically, you will learn how to underline, boldface, and center text as you're typing the text. In addition you will use block commands to change the way characters appear *after* you have typed them in. You will use block commands to underline, boldface, and change text to uppercase/lowercase.

Later in the session, you will use formatting commands that affect how the pages in the current document will be formatted. Specifically, you will learn how to indent text, change line spacing, change tab settings, and force a page break. Table 2.1 displays some of the WordPerfect formatting assumptions that are in effect unless you change them.

When you issue a formatting command—for example, to change the line spacing or tab settings—your document is affected downward from the current cursor position until another formatting command of the same type is encountered or the document ends.

Table 2.1	Page size	8-1/2" X 11" inches 66 lines per page 54 typed lines
WordPerfect 5.1 Formatting Assumptions	Top margin	1" (6 lines)
	Bottom margin	1" (6 lines)
	Left margin	1" (6 lines)
	Right margin	1" (6 lines)
	Page numbering	None
	Line spacing	Single-space, 6 lines per inch
	Font	Standard single-strike, 10 pitch (10 characters per inch)
	Tabs	Every 1/2" (5 spaces)
	Full justification	On; text appears evenly aligned on both margins when printed (not displayed)

Before proceeding, make sure the following are true:

1. You have access to WordPerfect 5.1.

2. Your Advantage Diskette is inserted in the drive. You will save your work onto the diskette and retrieve the files that have been created for you. (Note: The Advantage Diskette can be made by copying all the files off your instructor's Master Advantage Diskette onto a formatted diskette.)

CHARACTER FORMATTING COMMANDS

In this section you will insert a few titles at the top of the SALES.MAR document (Figure 2.1). In the process you will practice a number of different commands, including the FLUSH RIGHT command, the DATE command, the CENTER command, and the UNDERLINE and BOLD commands.

Figure 2.1

SALES.MAR

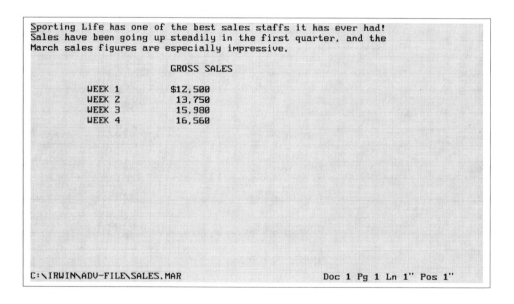

```
Sporting Life has one of the best sales staffs it has ever had!
Sales have been going up steadily in the first quarter, and the
March sales figures are especially impressive.

                    GROSS SALES

          WEEK 1       $12,500
          WEEK 2        13,750
          WEEK 3        15,980
          WEEK 4        16,560




C:\IRWIN\ADV-FILE\SALES.MAR                        Doc 1 Pg 1 Ln 1" Pos 1"
```

FLUSH RIGHT (Alt+F6) AND DATE (Shift+F5)

If you want text to appear on the right side of the page, against the right margin (such as the current date), use the **FLUSH RIGHT** (Alt+F6) command. *Using the menu bar, choose Flush Right from the Layout menu.* In this step you will use the FLUSH RIGHT command at the top of the document and then insert the current date using the **DATE** command (Shift+F5). *Using the menu bar, choose Date from the Tools menu.*

When using the DATE command, you have the option of inserting the date as text into the document, or as a code. If you decide to insert the date as a code, the current date will be inserted in the document every time you retrieve and/or print it. Note: If your computer isn't configured with a battery-powered clock, you may want to type the current date in rather than use the DATE command.

Perform the following steps:

1. Retrieve SALES.MAR from the Advantage Diskette.

2. Position the cursor at the top of the SALES document:
    PRESS: [Home], [Home]
    PRESS: [↑]

3. To insert a line at the top of the document:
    PRESS: [Enter]

4. To move the cursor to the top of the document:
    PRESS: [↑]

5. To use the FLUSH RIGHT command:
    PRESS: [Alt]+[F6]

6. To insert the current date:
    PRESS: [Shift]+[F5]

7. To insert the text for the current date:
    CHOOSE: Date Text
    The current date should be displaying up against the right margin.
    PRESS: [Enter]

Quick Reference
Flush Right
[Alt]+[F6]

1. PRESS: [Alt]+[F6]
2. TYPE: *the information you want to appear up against the right margin*

Quick Reference
Date
[Shift]+[F5]

1. PRESS: [Shift]+[F5]
2. If you want the date to be stored in the document as text:
    CHOOSE: Date Text
    If you want the date to be stored in the document as a code:
    CHOOSE: Date Code

CENTER (Shift+F6)

Centering involves positioning the cursor beneath the first character in the group of words that you want to center and then using the **CENTER** command (Shift+F6). *Using the menu bar, choose Center from the Layout menu.* To center text as you're typing it in, you must first use the CENTER command (which moves the cursor to the center of the text page) and then type in the text to be centered. To illustrate, you will insert a centered title at the top of the SALES.MAR document.

Perform the following steps:

1. To initiate the CENTER command:
   PRESS: Shift+F6

2. TYPE: SALES ARE UP!
   PRESS: Enter
   The screen should look like Figure 2.2.

Figure 2.2

The current date and a title have been inserted at the top of the SALES.MAR document.

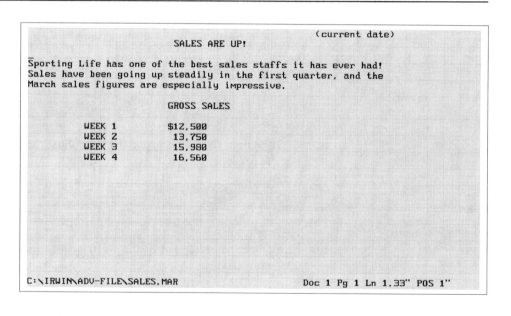

```
                                                      (current date)
                            SALES ARE UP!
 _
 Sporting Life has one of the best sales staffs it has ever had!
 Sales have been going up steadily in the first quarter, and the
 March sales figures are especially impressive.

               GROSS SALES

        WEEK 1        $12,500
        WEEK 2         13,750
        WEEK 3         15,980
        WEEK 4         16,560




 C:\IRWIN\ADV-FILE\SALES.MAR                  Doc 1 Pg 1 Ln 1.33" POS 1"
```

....

Quick Reference
Centering Text
Shift+F6

As you type text in:
1. PRESS: Shift+F6
2. TYPE: *the information you want centered*

After you have typed text in:
1. Position the cursor on the first character of text to be centered.
2. PRESS: Shift+F6

....

UNDERLINE (F8) AND BOLD (F6)

To **underline** text as you're typing it in, press F8 to begin underlining, type your text, and then press F8 to end underlining. To make text **bold** as you're typing it in, the same procedure is used but with F6. *To underline or boldface using the menu bar, choose Appearance from the Font menu, and then choose either Underline or Bold.* (Note: Underlining and boldfacing text *after* you've typed it in requires that you use a BLOCK command. Block commands are described in the next section.)

In this step you will insert an underlined and centered title at the top of the SALES document. Perform the following steps (the cursor should be one line below the current centered title):

1. To initiate the CENTER command:
   PRESS: Shift+F6

2. To initiate the UNDERLINE command:
   PRESS: F8
   Note the "Pos" indicator in the status area (lower right-hand corner). It should have changed in appearance now that you have pressed F8. (Depending on your monitor, it will appear either in a different color or underlined.)
   TYPE: (MARCH)

3. To end the UNDERLINE command:
   PRESS: F8
   PRESS: Enter

4. To see the codes that WordPerfect has embedded in your document, use the REVEAL CODES command:
   PRESS: Alt+F3 (*or* F11)
   The screen should look similar to Figure 2.3.

5. To turn the REVEAL CODES command off:
   PRESS: Alt+F3 (*or* F11)

COMBINING COMMANDS

What if you want some text in a document to appear both underlined and boldfaced? You simply press F8 and then F6 (it doesn't matter in which order), type in the text you want underlined and boldfaced, and then press F8 and F6 (again, it doesn't matter in which order). For practice, you will insert an underlined and boldfaced title (1993) near the top of your document. (The cursor should be positioned below the MARCH title.)

Figure 2.3

Revealing
codes. The
flush right,
center, and
underline
codes have
been ins-
erted in
your doc-
ument.

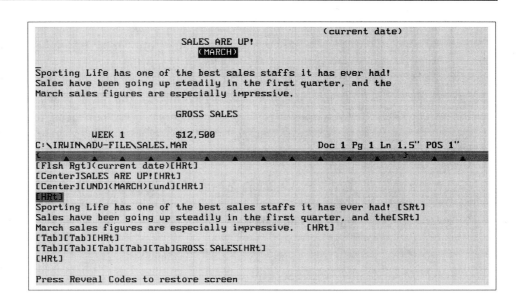

1. To initiate the CENTER command:
   PRESS: Shift+F6

2. To initiate the UNDERLINE command:
   PRESS: F8

3. To initiate the BOLD command:
   PRESS: F6

4. TYPE: 1993

5. To end the UNDERLINE and the BOLD commands:
   PRESS: F8
   PRESS: F6
   PRESS: Enter

6. To see the codes that WordPerfect has embedded in your document:
   PRESS: Alt+F3 (or F11)
   Note that there is an underline and bold code on each side of "1993."

7. To turn the REVEAL CODES command off:
   PRESS: Alt+F3 (or F11)

8. Save this document onto the Advantage Diskette as SALES.MAR. Make sure
   you replace the copy on disk with the updated copy in RAM.

Quick Reference	1. PRESS: F8 *to initiate underlining*
Underlining F8	2. TYPE: *the text you want to underline*
	3. PRESS: F8 *to end underlining*

Quick Reference	1. PRESS: F8 *to initiate boldfacing*
Boldfacing F6	2. TYPE: *the text you want to boldface*
	3. PRESS: F8 *to end boldfacing*

CHARACTER FORMATTING USING BLOCK COMMANDS

A **block** of text is composed of one or more characters in your document. Once text has been entered into a document, you can highlight blocks of text using the **BLOCK** command (Alt+F4) and then perform commands on them. If you are using a keyboard with 12 function keys, F12 can be used to initiate the BLOCK command. Using the BLOCK command involves the following steps, which you will work through in the next sections.

1. Position the cursor at the beginning of the block you want to perform a command on.

2. Initiate the BLOCK command (Alt+F4) (F12). The words "Block on" should blink in the bottom-left corner. *If you are using the menu bar, select Block from the Edit menu.*

3. Use the cursor-movement keys to highlight the block of text you want to perform a command on.

4. Perform a command on the highlighted block (for example, underline, bold, and so on).

HIGHLIGHTING BLOCKS

WordPerfect provides two different methods for highlighting blocks of text after the BLOCK command has been initiated: (a) You can highlight text using the cursor-movement keys, or (b) if you type a character, text will be highlighted until that character is encountered—for example, if you type a period (.), the sentence will be highlighted. To illustrate:

1. To clear the screen so you can work with another file:
    PRESS: [F7]
    CHOOSE: <u>N</u>o
    CHOOSE: <u>N</u>o

2. Retrieve the WPBLOCK.1 file from the Advantage Diskette.

3. To position the cursor on the first line of the first paragraph:
    PRESS: [↓]

4. To initiate the BLOCK command:
    PRESS: [Alt]+[F4] (*or* [F12])

5. To highlight the first word (After):
    PRESS: [→] *five times*

6. To highlight through the comma:
    TYPE: ,
    The screen should look like Figure 2.4.

Figure 2.4

Highlighting blocks. In this example, the BLOCK command was initiated and then a comma was typed.

```
Entering Text
After you have loaded your word processing software into RAM, the
next step is to enter, or key in, your text.  When entering text,
you will deal with (1) cursor movement, (2) word wrap and the Enter
key, (3) scrolling, and (4) formatting.
    In most word processing programs, the cursor is a blinking or
highlighted line (or block), about as wide as a character, that
marks where the next character will be entered or the starting
point of the next command operation.  As you type a character, the
cursor moves to the right.  You can control where the cursor is
positioned in order to edit text by using the cursor-movement keys
on your keyboard.
Block on                                  Doc 1 Pg 1 Ln 1.33" POS 7.1"
```

7. To highlight to the end of the sentence:
    TYPE: .

8. To highlight to the end of the paragraph:
    PRESS: [Enter]

9. To exit the BLOCK command, use the Cancel key (described in Session 1):
    PRESS: [F1]

....

Quick Reference   1. To initiate the BLOCK command:
Highlighting Blocks   PRESS: [Alt]+[F4] (*or* [F12])
                          2. To highlight a block, either use the cursor-movement keys or type a
                              character (text will be highlighted up to that character).

....

UNDERLINING ([F8]) AND BOLDFACING ([F6]) A BLOCK

In this section you will use the BLOCK command to underline all the headings in
the WPBLOCK.1 document. In addition you will make a few terms appear bold
when printed.

To underline the "Entering Text" section heading:

1. Position the cursor beneath the "E" of "Entering Text" at the top of the
    document.

2. To initiate the BLOCK command:
    PRESS: [Alt]+[F4] (*or* [F12])

3. To highlight and then underline the block:
    PRESS: [End], [F8]

To underline the "Editing Text" section heading:

1. Position the cursor beneath the "E" of "Editing Text."

2. To initiate the BLOCK command:
    PRESS: [Alt]+[F4] (*or* [F12])

3. To highlight and then underline the block:
    PRESS: [End], [F8]

....

Quick Reference   1. To initiate the BLOCK command:
Underlining a Block   PRESS: [Alt]+[F4] (*or* [F12])
                          2. Highlight the block that you want to underline.
                          3. To underline the block:
                              PRESS: [F8]

....

To underline the "Spell-Checking and the Thesaurus" section heading on page 4:

1. Position the cursor beneath the "S" of "Spell-Checking and the Thesaurus."

2. To initiate the BLOCK command:
    PRESS: `Alt`+`F4` (*or* `F12`)

3. To highlight and then underline the block:
    PRESS: `End`, `F8`

To underline the "Printing" section heading on page 5:

1. Position the cursor beneath the "P" of "Printing."

2. To initiate the BLOCK command:
    PRESS: `Alt`+`F4` (*or* `F12`)

3. To highlight and then underline the block:
    PRESS: `End`, `F8`

To boldface the word "cursor" located in the first line of the second paragraph of the Entering Text section:

1. Position the cursor beneath the "c" of "cursor."

2. To initiate the BLOCK command:
    PRESS: `Alt`+`F4` (*or* `F12`)

3. To highlight then boldface the block:
    PRESS: `Ctrl`+`→`
    PRESS: `F6`

....

Quick Reference
Boldfacing a Block

1. To initiate the BLOCK command:
    PRESS: `Alt`+`F4` (*or* `F12`)
2. Highlight the block that you want to boldface.
3. To boldface the block:
    PRESS: `F6`

....

To boldface the words "word wrap" located on the second line of the third paragraph:

1. Position the cursor beneath the "w" of "word"

2. To initiate the BLOCK command:
    PRESS: [Alt]+[F4] (*or* [F12])

3. To highlight the block:
    PRESS: [→] *nine times*

4. PRESS: [F6]

To boldface the word "scrolling" located on the first line of the fourth paragraph:

1. Position the cursor beneath the "s" of "scrolling."

2. To initiate the BLOCK command:
    PRESS: [Alt]+[F4] (*or* [F12])

3. To highlight the block:
    TYPE: g

4. PRESS: [F6]

UPPERCASE/LOWERCASE ([Alt]+[F4], [Shift]+[F3])

In this section you will change all the headings to uppercase (all capital letters) in the WPBLOCK.1 document. When the BLOCK command has been initiated ([Alt]+[F4]), the SWITCH command ([Shift]+[F3]) gives you the **Switch to Uppercase/Lowercase** function to change text from lowercase to uppercase, or vice versa.

To change to uppercase the "Entering Text" section heading:

1. Position the cursor beneath the "E" of "Entering Text" at the top of the document.

2. To initiate the BLOCK command:
    PRESS: [Alt]+[F4] (*or* [F12])

3. To highlight the block:
    PRESS: [End]

4. To change the highlighted block to uppercase:
    PRESS: [Shift]+[F3]
    WordPerfect is now displaying the Uppercase and Lowercase options on the bottom of the screen.
    CHOOSE: Uppercase

Quick Reference
Changing a Block to
Uppercase and
Lowercase

1. To initiate the BLOCK command:
   PRESS: Alt+F4 (*or* F12)
2. Highlight the block that you want to change to uppercase/lowercase.
3. To change the case:
   PRESS: Shift+F3
4. Choose either Uppercase or Lowercase.

To change to uppercase the "Editing Text" section heading:

1. Position the cursor beneath the "E" of "Editing Text."

2. To initiate the BLOCK command:
   PRESS: Alt+F4 (*or* F12)

3. To highlight the block:
   PRESS: End

4. To change the highlighted block to uppercase:
   PRESS: Shift+F3
   CHOOSE: Uppercase

To change to uppercase the "Spell-Checking and the Thesaurus" section heading on page 4:

1. Position the cursor beneath the "S" of "Spell-Checking and the Thesaurus."

2. To initiate the BLOCK command:
   PRESS: Alt+F4 (*or* F12)

3. To highlight the block:
   PRESS: End

4. To change the highlighted block to uppercase:
   PRESS: Shift+F3
   CHOOSE: Uppercase

To change to uppercase the "Printing" section heading:

1. Position the cursor beneath the "P" of "Printing."

2. To initiate the BLOCK command:
   PRESS: Alt+F4 (*or* F12)

3. To highlight the block:
   PRESS: End

4. To change the highlighted block to uppercase:
   PRESS: [Shift]+[F3]
   CHOOSE: Uppercase

5. Save (and replace) the WPBLOCK.1 document on the Advantage Diskette.

INDENTING

Indenting text is similar to changing a left or right margin, except that indent codes don't affect the entire document (you learn how to change margins in Session 4). Think of an indent code as a temporary margin change, because indent codes affect only paragraphs; that is, text conforms to the indent code only until you hit [Enter] (which inserts the [Enter] code, HRt, in the document). If a document needs a variety of margin changes, it may be easier to indent. WordPerfect allows you to **Indent** on the left margin ([F4]) or on both margins ([Shift]+[F4]). *Using the menu bar, choose Align from the Layout menu, and then choose Indent.*

In the next few sections, you will use indenting procedures to edit WPTEMP (Figure 2.5) to look like Figure 2.6. The sentence that begins with "The ideal room temperature" is indented along both margins 1-inch. The numbered points below are indented only along the left margin.

Figure 2.5

WPTEMP

```
Computer systems should be kept in an environment with as constant
a temperature as possible.  In cold climates, where office
temperatures are controlled by an automatic thermostat causing
warmer temperatures during the day and much cooler temperatures at
night, microcomputers tend to have the most system failures.  The
ideal room temperature for microcomputers ranges from 60 to 90
degrees Fahrenheit when the system is on and from 50 to 110 degrees
when the system is off.  But maintaining a constant temperature in
an environment is more important than the number of degrees.





C:\IRWIN\ADV-FILE\WPTEMP                          Doc 1 Pg 1 Ln 2.5" Pos 1"
```

Figure 2.6

The WPTEMP
document after
using indent
commands

```
Computer systems should be kept in an environment with as constant
a temperature as possible.  In cold climates, where office
temperatures are controlled by an automatic thermostat causing
warmer temperatures during the day and much cooler temperatures at
night, microcomputers tend to have the most system failures.
               The ideal room temperature for microcomputers
               ranges from 60 to 90 degrees Fahrenheit when
               the system is on and from 50 to 110 degrees
               when the system is off.
But maintaining a constant temperature in an environment is more
important than the number of degrees.  The following problems can
eventually occur if a microcomputer system is subjected to
substantial changes in temperature in short amounts of time:
1.   The chips inside the system unit can work their way out of
     their sockets in the system boards.  In addition, the chip
     connectors can corrode more quickly so that they become
     brittle and crack.
2.   Hard disks suffer from dramatic changes in temperature, which
     can cause read/write problems.  If a new hard disk drive has
     been shipped in a cold environment, manufacturers usually
     recommend that users wait for a few hours to a day before
     operating the hard disk.
These problems are caused by the expansion and contraction that
naturally occur when materials are heated and then cooled.  The
C:\IRWIN\DISKETTE\WPTEMP                            Doc 1 Pg 1 Ln 1" Pos 1"
```

To edit the first paragraph:

1. Clear the screen (F7, No, No) and then retrieve WPTEMP from the Advantage Diskette.

2. Position the cursor beneath the "T" of "The ideal room temperature."

3. PRESS: Enter

4. To indent the text along both margins 1 inch:
   PRESS: Shift+F4 *twice*

5. At this point, the rest of the paragraph is indented along both margins. To insert an HRt (hard return) code, or Enter code, after the first indented sentence, position the cursor beneath the "B" of "But maintaining."

6. PRESS: Enter
   The last sentence should now conform to the default margin settings (1-inch left, 1-inch right).

To add the new text and numbered points:

1. Position the cursor a few spaces to the right of the last sentence in this document.
   TYPE: The following problems can eventually occur if a microcomputer system is subjected to substantial changes in temperature in short amounts of time:
   PRESS: Enter

2. To type the first numbered point:
   TYPE: 1.
   PRESS: [F4]
   TYPE: The chips inside the system unit can work their way out of their sockets in the system boards. In addition, the chip connectors can corrode more quickly so that they become brittle and crack.
   PRESS: [Enter]

3. To type the second numbered point:
   TYPE: 2.
   PRESS: [F4]
   TYPE: Hard disks suffer from dramatic changes in temperature, which can cause read/write problems. If a new hard disk drive has been shipped in a cold environment, manufacturers usually recommend that users wait for a few hours to a day before operating the hard disk.
   PRESS: [Enter]

4. To finish the document:
   TYPE: These problems are caused by the expansion and contraction that naturally occur when materials are heated and then cooled. The bottom line is that changes in temperature are stressful for microcomputer systems.

5. With your cursor at the top of the document, your screen should look like Figure 2.6. Save the document as WPTEMP onto the Advantage Diskette. Make sure to "Replace" the file on disk with the updated contents of RAM.

Quick Reference
Indenting [F4]

Along the left margin:
1. PRESS: [F4]
2. TYPE: *the text you want indented*
3. PRESS: [Enter]

Along the left and right margins:
1. PRESS: [Shift]+[F4]
2. TYPE: *the text you want indented*
3. PRESS: [Enter]

CHANGING LINE SPACING (Shift+F8)

If you want to change the line spacing of an entire document, you must position the cursor at the top of the document before you insert the line-spacing code using the **FORMAT** command (Shift+F8), because formatting commands affect a document from the current cursor position downward. *(Using the menu bar, select Line from the Layout menu.)*

For example, if you want a paragraph in the middle of a document to be double-spaced, but the rest of the document to be single-spaced, you will have to issue two line-spacing commands. First, you would position the cursor at the beginning of the paragraph to be double-spaced. Then you would use the FORMAT command to change the spacing to double. This command will change not only the paragraph to be double-spaced, but also the rest of the document. And second, you would position the cursor at the beginning of the text (below the double-spaced paragraph) that you want single-spaced, and then use the FORMAT command to change the spacing to single from that point on.

In this section you will edit WPTEMP.2 to look like Figure 2.7. To double-space the entire document beginning with the indented text:

Figure 2.7

The line spacing of the second paragraph was changed to double by inserting a double-spacing code at the beginning of the second paragraph and a single-spacing code at the end of it.

```
Computer systems should be kept in an environment with as constant
a temperature as possible.  In cold climates, where office
temperatures are controlled by an automatic thermostat causing
warmer temperatures during the day and much cooler temperatures at
night, microcomputers tend to have the most system failures.

        The ideal room temperature for microcomputers

        ranges from 60 to 90 degrees Fahrenheit when

        the system is on and from 50 to 110 degrees

        when the system is off.

But maintaining a constant temperature in an environment is more
important than the number of degrees.  The following problems can
eventually occur if a microcomputer system is subjected to
substantial changes in temperature in short amounts of time:
1.    The chips inside the system unit can work their way out of
      their sockets in the system boards.  In addition, the chip
      connectors can corrode more quickly so that they become
      brittle and crack.            .
2.    Hard disks suffer from dramatic changes in temperature, which
      can cause read/write problems.  If a new hard disk drive has
C:\IRWIN\ADV-FILE\WPTEMP.Z                    Doc 1 Pg 1 Ln 3.33" Pos 1"
```

1.   Retrieve WPTEMP.2 from the Advantage Diskette.

2.   Position the cursor beneath the "T" of "The ideal room temperature."

3. To move the cursor to the left margin:
    PRESS: (Home), (←)

4. To insert a blank line:
    PRESS: (Enter)

5. To initiate the FORMAT command:
    PRESS: (Shift)+(F8)

6. CHOOSE: Line, Line Spacing

7. To specify double-spacing:
    TYPE: 2
    PRESS: (Enter)

8. To leave the Format menu and return to the document:
    PRESS: (F7)
    The screen should look like Figure 2.8. Note that everything below the cursor
    is double-spaced.

Figure 2.8

The document
is double-spaced
from the current
cursor position
downward.

```
Computer systems should be kept in an environment with as constant
a temperature as possible.  In cold climates, where office
temperatures are controlled by an automatic thermostat causing
warmer temperatures during the day and much cooler temperatures at
night, microcomputers tend to have the most system failures.

          The ideal room temperature for microcomputers

          ranges from 60 to 90 degrees Fahrenheit when

          the system is on and from 50 to 110 degrees

          when the system is off.

But maintaining a constant temperature in an environment is more

important than the number of degrees.  The following problems can

eventually occur if a microcomputer system is subjected to

substantial changes in temperature in short amounts of time:

1.    The chips inside the system unit can work their way out of

C:\IRWIN\ADV-FILE\WPTEMP.2                         Doc 1 Pg 1 Ln 2" Pos 1"
```

To single-space the rest of the document after the indented text:

1. Position the cursor beneath the "B" of "But maintaining."

2. To initiate the FORMAT command:
    PRESS: (Shift)+(F8)

3. CHOOSE: Line, Line Spacing

4. To specify single-spacing:
   TYPE: 1
   PRESS: [Enter]
   The screen should look like Figure 2.7.

5. To leave the Format menu and return to the document:
   PRESS: [F7]

6. Save the document as WPTEMP.2 onto the Advantage Diskette. Make sure you "Replace" the file on disk with the updated contents of RAM.

Quick Reference
Line Spacing
[Shift]+[F8]

1. Position the cursor where you want the spacing change to begin.
2. TYPE: [Shift]+[F8]
3. CHOOSE: Line, Line Spacing
4. TYPE: *a number that corresponds to the spacing you want*

CHANGING TAB SETTINGS ([Shift]+[F8])

WordPerfect automatically sets tabs—which are used to set up tabular material, such as a table—every 1/2-inch when you load the program. Not only can you set tabs in new locations but you can change the tab "type." The tabs set up by WordPerfect are all Left Tabs. Table 2.2 describes the five types of tabs you can set using WordPerfect. As when issuing other types of formatting codes, when you make a change in the tab line, the change affects the document from the current cursor position until another tab line is encountered or the document ends.

In this section you will create a small document named SALES (pictured in Figure 2.9) to practice changing the tab settings in a document (the top of the document has scrolled off the top of the screen). You will create a Left Tab and two Decimal Tabs that will be used for lining up text and numbers relating to the income and expenses of a sporting goods store named Sporting Life.

Specifically, you will perform the following activities:

1. Type in a paragraph using double-spacing.

2. Use the FORMAT command to change the tabs. *Using the menu bar, select Layout.*

3. Delete the current tab settings.

Table 2.2	<u>Type</u>	<u>Tab Line Symbol</u>	<u>Description</u>
Description of Different Tab Types	Left	L	The tab will remain to the left of the text you type. By default, WordPerfect sets Left Tabs every 1/2".
	Right	R	The tab will remain to the right of the text you type (similar to when the FLUSH RIGHT command is used).
	Center	C	The text you type will center on the tab position. This type of tab is used if text in a column needs to be centered.
	Decimal	D	The numbers you type will line up on the decimal. This type of tab is useful when you must type in columns of numbers.
	Dot Leader	.	You can make any tab a dot leader tab by typing a dot after typing in the tab line symbol. For example, you might type **R.** on the tab line. In your document, when you press (Tab), dots will fill in the space up to the Dot Leader Tab. This type of tab is useful when creating a table of contents.

Figure 2.9

SALES

```
reasonable prices.  It is also known for having helpful (not pushy)
salespeople who are knowledgeable about the items in the store.
Without all of you out on the floor, Sporting Life would be "just
another sporting goods store."  Keep up the good work!

                        INCOME          EXPENSES
            JAN      $89,100.90       $12,200.57
            FEB      125,200.00        15,100.90
            MAR      230,300.45        34,900.00
            APR      270,400.00        34,200.35
            MAY      410,500.50        52,700.00
            JUN      550,700.00        62,300.55

C:\IRWIN\DISKETTE\SALES                      Doc 1 Pg 1 Ln 5.33" Pos 1"
```

4. Set up the new tab settings.

5. Type in the table information.

6. Set up Left Tabs every 1/2-inch (as they were set originally).

Perform the following steps to change the line spacing and begin a new document:

1. To begin a new document:
    PRESS: F7
    CHOOSE: No, No

2. To initiate the FORMAT command so you can change the line spacing to double-spacing:
    PRESS: Shift + F8

3. To choose the Line option:
    CHOOSE: Line

4. To choose the Line Spacing option:
    CHOOSE: Line Spacing

5. To specify double-spacing:
    TYPE: 2
    PRESS: Enter

6. To leave the Format menu and return to the document:
    PRESS: F7

7. TYPE: It is my pleasure to announce to Sporting Life's sales staff that sales have been going up steadily for the past six months. As you know, Sporting Life is known for carrying quality sporting items at reasonable prices. It is also known for having helpful (not pushy) salespeople who are knowledgeable about the items in the store. Without all of you out on the floor, Sporting Life would be "just another sporting goods store." Keep up the good work!
    PRESS: Enter

Perform the following steps to change the tab settings in the document:

1. The cursor should be positioned below the paragraph you just typed (on the next line).

2. In this step you will type the headings for the table using the current tab settings.
   PRESS: [Tab] *five times*
   TYPE: INCOME
   PRESS: [Tab] *twice*
   TYPE: EXPENSES
   PRESS: [Enter]
   The cursor is now in the correct location (one line below the INCOME and EXPENSES headings) for changing the tabs (Figure 2.10).

Figure 2.10

The cursor is in the correct location for changing tabs.

```
It is my pleasure to announce to Sporting Life's sales staff that

sales have been going up steadily for the past six months.  As you

know, Sporting Life is known for carrying quality sporting items at

reasonable prices.  It is also known for having helpful (not pushy)

salespeople who are knowledgeable about the items in the store.

Without all of you out on the floor, Sporting Life would be "just

another sporting goods store."  Keep up the good work!
                    INCOME          EXPENSES

_

C:\IRWIN\DISKETTE\SALES                    Doc 1 Pg 1 Ln 3.67" Pos 1"
```

3. To initiate the FORMAT command:
   PRESS: [Shift]+[F8]

4. To choose the Line option:
   CHOOSE: Line

5. To choose the Tab Set option:
   CHOOSE: Tab Set
   The tab line should be displaying on the screen. On the tab line, position 0 is position 1 on the printed page. Therefore, if you set a tab in position 2.5, the tab is actually in position 3.5 on the printed page.

6. To delete the current tab settings so you can set new ones, you must first position the cursor on the left side of the tab line and then press [Ctrl]+[End]. Press the following keys:
   PRESS: [Home] *twice*
   PRESS: [←]
   PRESS: [Ctrl]+[End]

7. To set a Left Tab in position 1.5:
    TYPE: 1.5
    PRESS: [Enter]

8. To set a Decimal Tab in position 3:
    TYPE: 3
    PRESS: [Enter]
    TYPE: D

9. To set a Decimal Tab in position 4.5:
    TYPE: 4.5
    PRESS: [Enter]
    TYPE: D

10. To leave the Format menu and return to the document:
    PRESS: [F7] *twice*

Now you will type in the table information:

1. PRESS: [Tab]
    TYPE: JAN
    PRESS: [Tab]
    TYPE: $89,100.90
    PRESS: [Tab]
    TYPE: $12,200.57
    PRESS: [Enter]

2. PRESS: [Tab]
    TYPE: FEB
    PRESS: [Tab]
    TYPE: 125,200.00
    PRESS: [Tab]
    TYPE: 15,100.90
    PRESS: [Enter]

3. Continue until all the expenses information for the six months has been entered (refer to Figure 2.9). After you have typed in the last expenses amount (62,300.55):
    PRESS: [Enter]
    The document should look like Figure 2.9.

To reset tabs in every 1/2-inch (this is how they were set before you changed them):

1. Position the cursor at the bottom of the document (below the table):
    PRESS: [Home], [Home]
    PRESS: [↓]

2. To initiate the FORMAT command:
    PRESS: [Shift]+[F8]

3. CHOOSE: Line
    CHOOSE: Tab Set

4. To clear the current tab line:
    PRESS: [Home] *twice*
    PRESS: [←]
    PRESS: [Ctrl]+[End]

5. To set a left tab every 1/2-inch:
    TYPE: 0,.5
    PRESS: [Enter]

6. To leave the Format menu and return to the document:
    PRESS: [F7] *twice*

7. Save this document onto the Advantage Diskette as SALES.

....

Quick Reference   Clearing tabs:
Tab Settings   1. PRESS: [Shift]+[F8]
[Shift]+[F8]   2. To choose the Line option:
                               CHOOSE: Line
                           3. To choose the Tab Set option:
                               CHOOSE: Tab Set
                           4. Position the cursor on the left side of the tab line:
                               PRESS: [Home], [Home], [←]
                           5. To clear the tabs:
                               PRESS: [Ctrl]+[End]

                           Setting new tabs:
                           1. After initiating the FORMAT command
                               CHOOSE: Line, Tab Set
                               TYPE: *the number that corresponds to the place on the tab line where you want to position a tab*
                               PRESS: [Enter]
                           2. TYPE: *a letter (L, R, D, C) that corresponds to the type of tab you are setting*

....

Quick Reference
Tab Settings
[Shift]+[F8]
(concluded)

Resetting tabs to every 1/2-inch:
1. After initiating the FORMAT command:
    CHOOSE: Line, Tab Set
2. Position the cursor on the left side of the tab line:
    PRESS: [Home], [Home], [←]
3. Clear the current tab settings.
4. TYPE: 0, .5
    PRESS: [Enter]

FORCING A PAGE BREAK ([Ctrl]+[Enter])

Many documents require that only a small amount of information appear on a page. For example, what if you want to include a title page? Or what if you want a table to appear alone on a page for clarity and emphasis? You can force a page break (that is, start a new page) by first positioning the cursor where you want the new page to begin and then holding [Ctrl] down and pressing [Enter]. In this section you will use the **Force Page Break** option so that the table you created in the last section is on a separate page. We will then show you how to delete the page break.

Perform the following steps:

1. Position the cursor one character to the right of the last line of the paragraph located above the table ("Keep up the good work!").

2. To insert a page break:
    PRESS: [Ctrl]+[Enter]
    Note that the cursor is now on page 2 (Figure 2.11). If you were to print the SALES document right now, the table would print out at the top of page 2.

3. To see the code you just inserted in your document, use the REVEAL CODES command:
    PRESS: [Alt]+[F3] (*or* [F11])
    You should see the hard page code HPg to the right of the word "work!". (When WordPerfect begins a new page on its own, a "soft page" (SPg) code is inserted in your document.)

4. To delete the HPg code, position the cursor to the right of the code and press Backspace or highlight the code and press Delete. The table should again be on page 1.

Figure 2.11

A page break
has been ins-
erted in the
SALES
document.

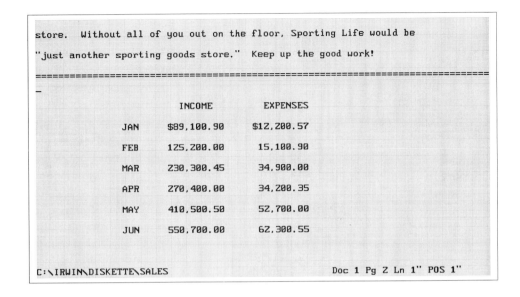

```
store.  Without all of you out on the floor, Sporting Life would be

"just another sporting goods store."  Keep up the good work!

====================================================================
_

                    INCOME          EXPENSES

            JAN     $89,100.90      $12,200.57

            FEB     125,200.00      15,100.90

            MAR     230,300.45      34,900.00

            APR     270,400.00      34,200.35

            MAY     410,500.50      52,700.00

            JUN     550,700.00      62,300.55


C:\IRWIN\DISKETTE\SALES                      Doc 1 Pg 2 Ln 1" POS 1"
```

5. To leave the Reveal Codes screen and return to your document:
   PRESS: [Alt]+[F3] (*or* [F11])

SUMMARY

In this session you used character-formatting commands to change the way characters display in your documents. Specifically, you learned how to underline, boldface, and center text as you're typing the text. Block commands are used to change the way characters appear *after* you have typed them in. You used block commands to underline, boldface, and change text to uppercase/lowercase.

Later in the session, you used page-formatting commands that affect how the pages in the current document will be formatted. Specifically, you learned how to indent text, change line spacing, change tab settings, and force a page break using [Ctrl]+[Enter].

Remember that, when issuing a formatting command—for example, to change the line spacing or tab settings—your document is affected downward from the current cursor position until another formatting command of the same type is encountered or the document ends.

COMMAND SUMMARY

The following table provides a list of the commands and procedures covered in this session.

Table 2.3	[Alt]+[F6]	Flush right
Command Summary	[Shift]+[F5], Date Text or Date Code	Insert the current date in a document
	[Shift]+[F6]	Center
	[F8], type text, [F8]	Underline text as you're typing it in
	[F6], type text, [F6]	Boldface text as you're typing it in
	[Alt]+[F4], highlight a block, [F8]	Underline a block
	[Alt]+[F4], highlight a block, [F6]	Boldface a block
	[Alt]+[F4], highlight a block, [Shift]+[F3], Uppercase/Lowercase	Change a block of text from upper-case to lowercase and vice-versa
	[F4]	Indent text along the left margin
	[Shift]+[F4]	Indent text along both margins
	[Shift]+[F8], Line, Line Spacing, type line spacing #, [Enter]	Change line spacing
	[Shift]+[F8], Line, Tab Set, [Home], [Home], [←], [Ctrl]+[End]	Clear the current tab settings
	[Shift]+[F8], Line, Tab Set, type tab position #, [Enter], type a tab letter	Set new tabs
	[Shift]+[F8], Line, Tab Set, [Home], [Home], [←], type 0, .5, [Enter]	Reset tabs to every 1/2"
	[Ctrl]+[Enter]	Insert a hard page break

KEY TERMS

Block (Alt+F4)(F12)) This command enables the user to perform commands (underline, boldface, center, and so on) on more than one character at a time.

Bold (F6)) This command enables you to make text appear darker when printed.

Center (Shift+F6)) This command enables you to center text between the margins before or after it has been typed in.

Date (Shift+F5)) This key is used to copy the system date into a document. The user has the option of copying the date into the document as text or as a code.

Flush Right (Alt+F6)) This key enables the user to align characters against the right margin.

Force Page Break (Ctrl+Enter)) This command enables you to insert a page break in the middle of a document. Anything that follows the page break will display on the top of the next page.

Format (Shift+F8)) This key is used to provide you with options for changing the way your documents are formatted. For example, with this key you can change margins or line spacing and include headers and footers.

Indent (F4); Shift+F4)) These commands let you insert temporary margin changes in your documents. The INDENT command is in effect until a hard return is encountered in your document.

Switch to Uppercase/Lowercase (Alt+F4, Shift+F3)) This command enables you to change the case of a block of characters from uppercase to lowercase, and vice versa.

Underline (F8)) This command enables you to display text so that it is underlined when printed.

EXERCISES

SHORT ANSWER

1. What is the importance of cursor position when you use formatting commands in a document?
2. What is the main difference between indenting text and changing the margins?
3. When creating a document, why might you want to make a change to the tab line?

4. What procedure would you follow to underline a few words? Boldface?
5. When you first load WordPerfect, what are the assumptions made by WordPerfect about tabs? What about line spacing?
6. Describe the procedure for highlighting a block and then underlining it.
7. You're formatting a document that contains three paragraphs. If your objective is to change the line spacing for the second paragraph to double-spacing, how many line-spacing commands will you have to issue?
8. What procedure would you follow to center a title after it has been typed in?
9. To change the line spacing in an entire document, where must you position the cursor?
10. What is the function of the PAGE BREAK command? When might you want to use it?

HANDS-ON

1. In this exercise you will use the FLUSH RIGHT and DATE commands and change line spacing. Retrieve HARDWARE from the Advantage Diskette. Perform the following tasks:
   a. Insert your underlined name on the first line of the document against the right margin (use the FLUSH RIGHT command).
   b. Insert the current date using the FLUSH RIGHT and DATE commands on the second line of the document.
   c. Insert the following centered title two lines below the current date: MICROCOMPUTER HARDWARE OVERVIEW
   d. Insert one blank line below the centered title.
   e. Change the spacing of the first paragraph to double-spacing. The rest of the document should remain single-spaced.
   f. Save the document onto the Advantage Diskette.
   g. Print HARDWARE.

2. Create the document pictured in Figure 2.12.
   a. Insert your name at the top of the document and then boldface it.
   b. Do what it says on each line. For example, center the line that says "This line is centered."
   c. Save this document onto the Advantage Diskette as PRACTICE.DOC.
   d. Print the document.

3. To practice revealing and then deleting codes from a document, retrieve CODES.DOC from the Advantage Diskette. Codes have been inserted into the document to make a number of words in this document appear underlined and boldfaced. In addition, a line-spacing code has been inserted in the document. Delete all underline, bold, and line-spacing codes from the document. Print the document.

Figure 2.12

PRACTICE.DOC

```
This line is centered
This line is boldfaced
This line is underlined
Boldface and underline this text
Make this text appear in the Flush Right position
Insert the current date here
Center the current date between the margins
Insert the current date in the Flush Right position
Underline and center this text
Boldface and right align this text




                                                   Doc 1 Pg 1 Ln 1" Pos 1"
```

4. In this exercise you will practice setting new tabs in the BUDGET document. Retrieve BUDGET from the Advantage Diskette, and then perform the following steps:

    a. Position the cursor below the first paragraph.
    b. Clear the tab line.
    c. Set the following tabs, and then type in the data below (use `Tab` to line up the table information):
        (1) Center Tab in position 2.5.
        (2) Decimal Tab in position 4.
        (3) Decimal Tab in position 5.

	1992	1993
Los Angeles	546	710
San Francisco	672	980
Chicago	487	750
New York	1047	1200

    d. After typing in the data, set the tabs back to Left Tabs every 1/2-inch.
    e. Save BUDGET onto the Advantage Diskette.
    f. Print BUDGET.

5. In this exercise you will practice setting tabs to align a table of numbers. Perform the following steps:

    a. Clear the screen.
    b. Clear the tab line.
    c. Set the following tabs, and then type in the data below (use `Tab` to line up the table information):
        (1) Decimal Tab in position 2.5.
        (2) Decimal Tab in position 4.
        (3) Decimal Tab in position 5.

```
                January         February        March
   East         50,000.00       65,000.00       75,000.00
   West        125,000.00      105,000.00      100,500.00
   Central      55,000.00       50,000.00       75,000.00
```

d. After typing in the table information, press (Enter) three times.
e. TYPE: These are the forecasted commissions for the first part of 1993. Please add a discussion of these figures to the Sales Planning agenda next week.
f. Save this document as FORECAST onto the Advantage Diskette.

6. To practice indenting text in a document, create the document pictured below. (Note: Your document may look slightly different because the text in your document will wrap to the next line at a different point.) Save the document onto the Advantage Diskette as PROGRAMS.2. Print PROGRAMS.2.

LANGUAGE PROCESSORS

Computers understand only one language -- machine language "written" using the digits 1 and 0. Because it is too time-consuming to write programs in machine language, **high-level programming languages** were developed that are easier to learn and use.

With high-level languages, programmers don't have to use 1s and 0s to represent computer instructions. Instead they use everyday text and mathematical formulas which enable them to use fewer instructions per program.

>   Programs written using high-level languages still have to be converted into machine language before the computer "understands" them.

When programmers update programs by adding or improving features, they edit the high-level language version of the program. When finished, they use a language processor to create another machine language version of the program. Two types of language processors are used today: compilers and interpreters.

1. The **compiler** is a language processor that translates an entire high-level language program, referred to as source code, into a machine language version of the program, called the object code, in a single process.

2. The **interpreter** is a language processor that converts and executes high-level language instructions one instruction statement at a time.

7. To practice using block commands, retrieve the NAMES file from the Advantage Diskette and perform the following commands:
   a. Insert your name and address as the first name in the list.
   b. Boldface all names in the document (*don't* boldface the address, city, or zip information).
   c. Underline and center the second and fourth names in the list.
   d. Underline and right-align the third and fifth names in the list.
   e. Change to uppercase the second and third names in the list.
   f. Save this file onto the Advantage Diskette as NAMES.2.
   g. Print NAMES.2.

8. This exercise involves changing the tab line to include a right-aligned dot leader tab in position 6.5 inch.
   a. Create the following document and then save the document as AGENDA onto the Advantage Diskette:

```
              SALES PLANNING AGENDA

DATE:   April 4th, 1993 .............TIME: 9am-4pm

Who is our Customer?
    Demographic Analysis.................9:00-9:45am
    Psychographic Analysis.............9:50-10:30am
    Lifestyles and AIO Study...........10:45-12noon

What are we Selling?
    Research and Development............1:00-2:00pm
    Product Packaging..................2:05-2:45pm
    Pricing Structures.................3:00-3:30pm

Incentives and Commissions ...........3:35-4:00pm

Please be prepared to give a ten minute impromptu
presentation on the status of your department.

                    Your faithful V.P. of Marketing,

                                        your name
```

   b. Boldface the first two lines of the agenda including the title, date, and time.
   c. Boldface the three main agenda items.
   d. Underline the word "faithful" in the closing of the document.
   e. Include your name in the closing of the document.
   f. Save and then print AGENDA.

9. Create a document describing a course you want to take that includes the following:
   a. A tab change.
   b. Paragraph indents.
   c. A centered title.
   d. Your name and the current date.
   e. Boldfacing.
   f. Underlining.
   g. Double-spacing in a portion of the document.

   Save the document onto the Advantage Diskette and give the document the name of your choice. Print the document.

10. Pretend it is now five years in the future. Use WordPerfect to create a résumé that includes the following information about you: current career objectives, work experience, educational experience, special interests, volunteer activities, and so forth. You may want to organize the résumé chronologically beginning with your most recent work experience. You will probably want to perform the following types of tasks:
    a. Center and boldface your name, address, and phone number at the top of the document.
    b. Capitalize and boldface any titles that appear in the résumé (for example, the titles for OBJECTIVE, EDUCATION, WORK EXPERIENCE).
    c. Indent any descriptions you include (for example, the description of a job you held in the summer of 1990).
    d. Use underlining and boldfacing for emphasis.
    e. Save this document onto the Advantage Diskette as RESUME.2.
    f. Print RESUME.2.

SESSION 3

EDITING AND PROOFING
A DOCUMENT

One of the main reasons word processing software is so popular is that it enables you to easily change the text you've already typed. With minimal effort you can move, copy, delete, and search for text in a document. In addition, you can check for spelling errors and use a thesaurus to find the "perfect" word.

PREVIEW

When you have completed this session, you will be able to:

Work with more than one document at once.
·
Use the MOVE command.
·
Edit using block operations.
·
Search for and replace text.
·
Spell-check a document.
·
Use the thesaurus.

Why Is This Session Important?
Working with Two Documents (`Shift`+`F3`)
    Sizing the Windows
The MOVE Command (`Ctrl`+`F4`)
    Using the MOVE Command to Copy
    Using the MOVE Command to Delete
Editing Using Block Operations
    Moving and Copying a Block
    Deleting a Block
    Saving a Block
Searching for (`F2`) and Replacing (`Alt`+`F2`)
  Text
    Searching for Text
    Replacing Text
Spell-Checking a Document (`Ctrl`+`F2`)
Thesaurus (`Alt`+`F1`)
Summary
    Command Summary
Key Terms
Exercises
    Short Answer
    Hands-On

WHY IS THIS SESSION IMPORTANT?

This session gives you practice using a number of WordPerfect's editing commands. You will use a file named DETAIL.93 and a file named WPBLOCK.3 to practice the following:

1. Working with more than one document at a time.

2. Moving and copying blocks of text.

3. Searching for and replacing text.

In addition, you will use a file called WPSPELL (on the Advantage Diskette) to practice the following:

4. Using the spelling checker.

5. Using the thesaurus.

Before proceeding, make sure the following are true:

1. You have access to WordPerfect 5.1.

2. Your Advantage Diskette is inserted in the drive. You will save your work onto the diskette and retrieve the files that have been created for you. (Note: The Advantage Diskette can be made by copying all the files off your instructor's Master Advantage Diskette onto a formatted diskette.)

WORKING WITH TWO DOCUMENTS (Shift+F3)

A particularly useful feature of WordPerfect is its ability to store two documents in RAM at the same time. This feature makes it easy to copy or move text from one document to another, or to simply refer to text in another document. So far in this guide, you have been working only in the Doc 1 window. To work in the Doc 2 window, the **SWITCH** command (Shift+F3) is used. *Using the menu bar, select Switch from the Edit menu.*

The Doc 1 and Doc 2 windows function independently, therefore any command you use in one window will not affect the other. You can exit either window at any time. If you exit WordPerfect while both windows are open, or in use, WordPerfect will display a reminder message and prompt you to save each document.

In this section you will retrieve a copy of DETAIL.93 (stored on the Advantage Diskette) into the Doc 2 window and practice switching between windows. In a later section, we lead you through copying and moving summary information from the Doc 2 window into the Doc 1 window.

Perform the following steps:

1. The cursor should be positioned in the Doc 1 window, as indicated by the status information on the bottom of the screen. To clear any information that may be displaying in the Doc 1 window:
   PRESS: [F7]
   CHOOSE: No, No

2. To switch into the Doc 2 window:
   PRESS: [Shift]+[F3]
   You should see the designation "Doc 2" in the status area at the bottom of the screen.

3. Retrieve a copy of the DETAIL.93 file from your Advantage Diskette. The screen should look like Figure 3.1.

Figure 3.1

DETAIL.93

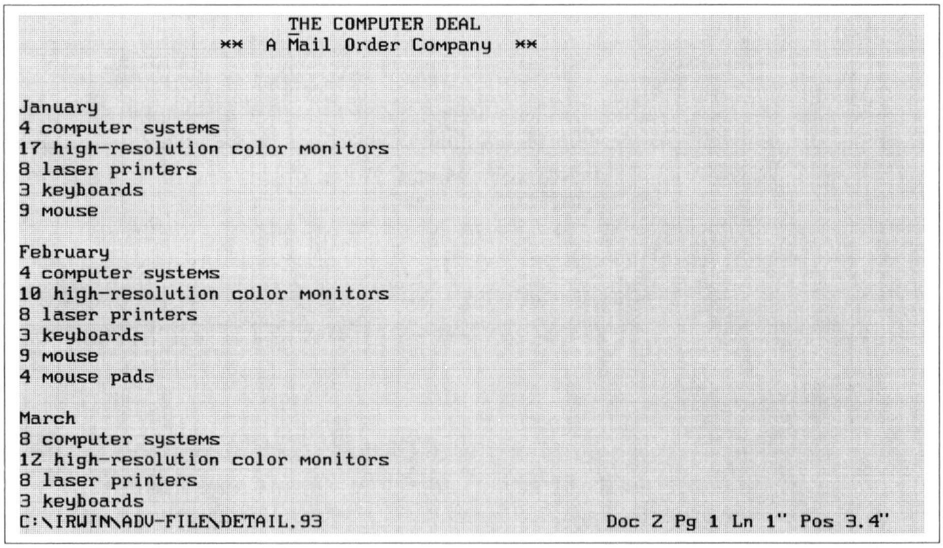

```
                      THE COMPUTER DEAL
              ** A Mail Order Company  **


January
4 computer systems
17 high-resolution color monitors
8 laser printers
3 keyboards
9 mouse

February
4 computer systems
10 high-resolution color monitors
8 laser printers
3 keyboards
9 mouse
4 mouse pads

March
8 computer systems
12 high-resolution color monitors
8 laser printers
3 keyboards
C:\IRWIN\ADV-FILE\DETAIL.93                    Doc 2 Pg 1 Ln 1" Pos 3.4"
```

4. DETAIL.93 is now in the Doc 2 window. To switch between the Doc 1 and Doc 2 windows:
   PRESS: [Shift]+[F3]

5. The Doc 1 window should now be displaying. To switch back to the Doc 2 window:
   PRESS: [Shift]+[F3]

If at this point you wanted to clear the document from the Doc 2 window, you would first switch into it and then use the EXIT command (F7). Since you will be using the information stored in the Doc 2 window in the next few sections, you won't perform the exit procedure now.

Quick Reference   To switch between the Doc 1 and Doc 2 windows:
Switch Shift+F3   PRESS: Shift+F3

SIZING THE WINDOWS

If you want to see the Doc 1 and Doc 2 windows on the screen at the same time, use the **WINDOW** command (Ctrl+F3). *Using the menu bar, choose Window from the Edit menu.* Unless you use the WINDOW command, each document window takes up 24 lines. To split the screen so that the Doc 1 and Doc 2 windows can both be viewed on the screen, perform the following steps:

1. PRESS: Ctrl+F3
    CHOOSE: Window
    TYPE: 12
    PRESS: Enter
    The screen should look like Figure 3.2. The screen is divided by a bar that separates the Doc 1 window on the top from the Doc 2 window on the bottom. The tab indicators on the bar separator point to the window the cursor is in. To switch between the screens, use the SWITCH command (Shift+F3), and note that the tab indicators change.

Figure 3.2

The screen has been divided into two windows.

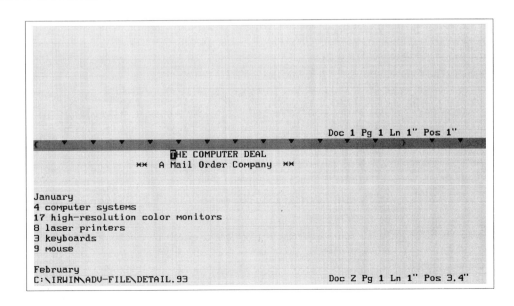

```
                                                        Doc 1 Pg 1 Ln 1" Pos 1"
⌐  ▼    ▼     ▼    ▼     ▼    ▼    ▼    ▼    ▼     ▼    ⌐      ▼    ▼
                         THE COMPUTER DEAL
                    ** A Mail Order Company  **

January
4 computer systems
17 high-resolution color monitors
8 laser printers
3 keyboards
9 mouse

February
C:\IRWIN\ADV-FILE\DETAIL.93                        Doc 2 Pg 1 Ln 1" Pos 3.4"
```

2. To enlarge each window back to 24 lines:
    PRESS: [Ctrl]+[F3]
    CHOOSE: Window
    TYPE: 24
    PRESS: [Enter]

....

1. PRESS: [Ctrl]+[F3]
2. CHOOSE: Window
3. Type in a number that corresponds to how large you want to make the current window.
    PRESS: [Enter]

....

THE MOVE COMMAND ([Ctrl]+[F4])

Although the command used in this section is called the **MOVE** command ([Ctrl]+[F4]), it also enables you to copy and delete. In addition, the APPEND option enables you to copy text to the end of another file stored on disk. Using the MOVE command involves the following steps, which you will practice in the next section:

1. Position the cursor at the beginning of the block (sentence, paragraph, or page) you want to perform a command on.

2. Initiate the MOVE command ([Ctrl]+[F4]). *Using the menu bar, choose Move from the Edit menu.*

3. Choose Sentence, Paragraph, or Page.

4. Choose the option that corresponds to one of the following:

    -   Move: This option enables you to select a sentence, paragraph, or page to be moved. Move the cursor to where the text should be moved, and press [Enter].

    -   Copy: This option enables you to select a sentence, paragraph, or page to be copied. Move the cursor to where the text should be copied, and press [Enter]. The original text remains intact.

    -   Delete: This option enables you to delete a sentence, paragraph, or page.

- Append: This option enables you to copy a sentence, paragraph, or page to the end of another file stored on disk. WordPerfect will ask you for the name of the file to append to. Type the filename and press (Enter).

USING THE MOVE COMMAND TO COPY

In this section you will work with the DETAIL.93 file that is currently stored in the Doc 2 window. The Doc 1 window should be empty at this point. Specifically, you will copy the 1st quarter summary paragraph and then the 2nd quarter summary paragraph into the Doc 1 window.

Perform the following steps to copy the 1st quarter summary paragraph into the Doc 1 window:

1. If your cursor is in the Doc 1 window, switch into the Doc 2 window using the SWITCH command ((Shift)+(F3)).

2. Using the cursor-movement keys, move the cursor to the beginning of the paragraph that summarizes the 1st quarter. The cursor should be positioned beneath the "1" of "1st."

3. To initiate the MOVE command:
   PRESS: (Ctrl)+(F4)
   The screen should look like Figure 3.3. (The Move menu is at the bottom of the screen.)

Figure 3.3

The Move
menu

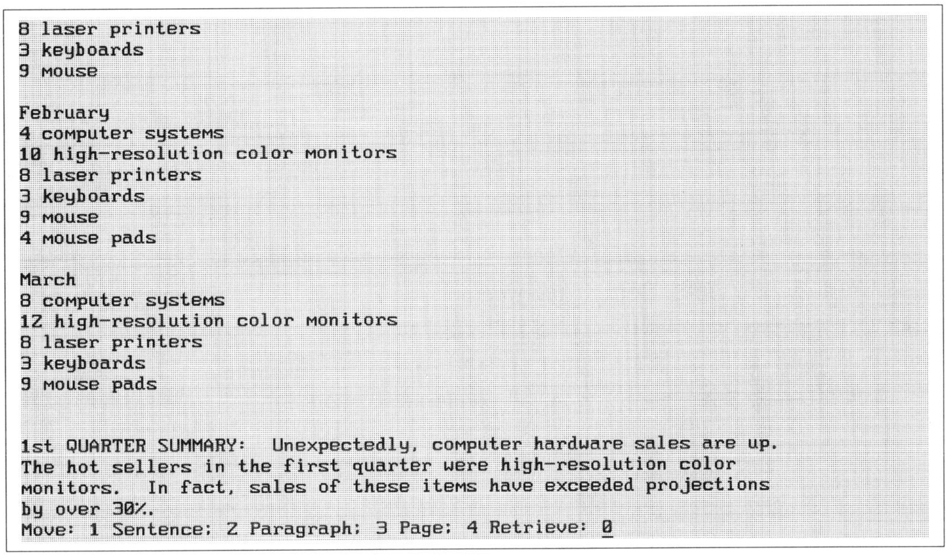

```
8 laser printers
3 keyboards
9 mouse

February
4 computer systems
10 high-resolution color monitors
8 laser printers
3 keyboards
9 mouse
4 mouse pads

March
8 computer systems
12 high-resolution color monitors
8 laser printers
3 keyboards
9 mouse pads


1st QUARTER SUMMARY:  Unexpectedly, computer hardware sales are up.
The hot sellers in the first quarter were high-resolution color
monitors.  In fact, sales of these items have exceeded projections
by over 30%.
Move: 1 Sentence; 2 Paragraph; 3 Page; 4 Retrieve: 0
```

4. To choose the Paragraph option:
    CHOOSE: Paragraph
    The 1st quarter summary paragraph should be highlighted.

5. To choose the Copy option:
    CHOOSE: Copy
    As the message indicates on the bottom-left corner of the screen, WordPerfect is now waiting for you to move the cursor to where you want the paragraph to be copied.

6. Move the cursor into the Doc 1 window.
    PRESS: Shift + F3

7. To retrieve the text:
    PRESS: Enter
    The screen should look like Figure 3.4.

Figure 3.4

A paragraph has been copied into the Doc 1 window.

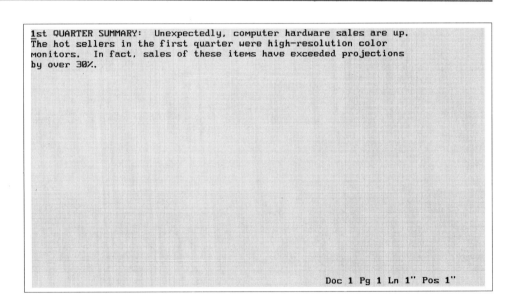

```
1st QUARTER SUMMARY:  Unexpectedly, computer hardware sales are up.
The hot sellers in the first quarter were high-resolution color
monitors.  In fact, sales of these items have exceeded projections
by over 30%.




                                                    Doc 1 Pg 1 Ln 1" Pos 1"
```

Perform the following steps to copy the 2nd quarter summary paragraph into the Doc 1 window:

1. If your cursor is in the Doc 1 window, switch into the Doc 2 window using the SWITCH command (Shift + F3).

2. Using the cursor-movement keys, move the cursor to the beginning of the paragraph that summarizes the 2nd quarter. The cursor should be positioned beneath the "2" of "2nd."

3. To initiate the MOVE command:
   PRESS: `Ctrl`+`F4`

4. CHOOSE: <u>P</u>aragraph
   The 2nd quarter summary paragraph should be highlighted.

5. CHOOSE: <u>C</u>opy
   WordPerfect is now waiting for you to move the cursor to where you want the paragraph to be copied.

6. To move the cursor into the Doc 1 window:
   PRESS: `Shift`+`F3`

7. To move the cursor to the bottom of the document:
   PRESS: `Home`, `Home`
   PRESS: `↓`

8. To retrieve the text:
   PRESS: `Enter`
   The 2nd quarter summary paragraph has now been copied into the Doc 1 window.

Quick Reference
Moving or Copying a Sentence, Paragraph, or Page
`Ctrl`+`F4`

1. To initiate the MOVE command:
   PRESS: `Ctrl`+`F4`
2. Choose the option that corresponds to either (1) Sentence, (2) Paragraph, or (3) Page.
3. Choose Move or Copy.
4. Move the cursor to where the text should be moved.
5. To move the text:
   PRESS: `Enter`

USING THE MOVE COMMAND TO DELETE

To show you how to delete text using the MOVE command, you will now delete the second paragraph in the Doc 1 window:

1. The cursor should be positioned in the Doc 1 window.

2. Position the cursor at the beginning of the second paragraph.

3. To initiate the MOVE command:
   PRESS: `Ctrl`+`F4`

4. CHOOSE: Paragraph, Delete
    The paragraph should have disappeared from the document.

5. To clear out of the Doc 1 window without saving:
    PRESS: [F7]
    CHOOSE: No, Yes
    You should now be viewing the DETAIL.93 document in the Doc 2 window.

It is actually easier to delete a paragraph or block of text using the BLOCK DELETE command, which we will describe shortly.

Quick Reference
Deleting a
Sentence,
Paragraph,
or Page
[Ctrl]+[F4]

1. To initiate the MOVE command:
    PRESS: [Ctrl]+[F4]
2. Choose the option that corresponds to either (1) Sentence, (2) Paragraph, or (3) Page.
3. To choose the Delete option:
    CHOOSE: Delete

EDITING USING BLOCK OPERATIONS

Whereas the MOVE command enables you to move and copy blocks of text in the form of sentences, paragraphs, and pages, the BLOCK command enables you to work with text of any amount. The procedure involves first using the block command ([Alt]+[F4]) to highlight a block of text, and then using the MOVE command ([Ctrl]+[F4]). (Note: Highlighting blocks was described in Session 2.)

In this section you learn how to move and copy using the BLOCK command. In addition you learn how to delete and save blocks of text.

MOVING AND COPYING A BLOCK

In this section you will use the BLOCK command to copy the January–March and 1st QUARTER SUMMARY information from the Doc 2 window into the Doc 1 window.

1. The cursor should be in the Doc 2 window. The DETAIL.93 document should be displaying on the screen.

2. Position the cursor at the top of the document:
    PRESS: [Home], [Home]

PRESS: ↑
The cursor should be positioned beneath the first character of the title.

3. To initiate the BLOCK command:
    PRESS: Alt + F4

4. To highlight the monthly and summary data, press ↓ until it is all highlighted. The screen should look like Figure 3.5.

Figure 3.5

The 1st quarter data has been highlighted us-ing the BLOCK command.

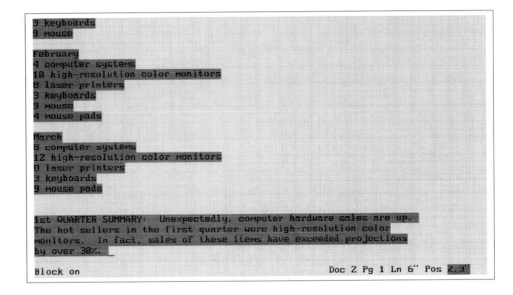

5. To copy the text into the Doc 1 window:
    PRESS: Ctrl + F4 (*or* F12)
    Note that one of the available options is Block.
    CHOOSE: Block, Copy

6. WordPerfect now wants to know where to copy the text. Since you are copying the text into the Doc 2 window:
    PRESS: Shift + F3

7. Since the cursor is now positioned where the text should be copied:
    PRESS: Enter
    Note that the title appears against the left margin because the center code wasn't included in the copied block (Figure 3.6).

Figure 3.6

The 1st quarter
data has been
copied into the
Doc 1 window.

```
THE COMPUTER DEAL
**  A Mail Order Company  **

January
4 computer systems
17 high-resolution color monitors
8 laser printers
3 keyboards
9 mouse

February
4 computer systems
10 high-resolution color monitors
8 laser printers
3 keyboards
9 mouse
4 mouse pads

March
8 computer systems
12 high-resolution color monitors
8 laser printers
3 keyboards
                                        Doc 1 Pg 1 Ln 1" Pos 1"
```

Quick Reference
Copying a Block

1. To initiate the BLOCK command:
   PRESS: [Alt]+[F4] (*or* [F12])
2. Highlight the block you want to copy.
3. To initiate the MOVE command:
   PRESS: [Ctrl]+[F4]
4. CHOOSE: Block, Copy
5. Move the cursor to where you want the block to be copied.
6. To copy the block:
   PRESS: [Enter]

DELETING A BLOCK

In this section you will use the BLOCK command to delete the titles at the top of
the text displaying in the Doc 1 window.

1. Position the cursor at the top of the document:
   PRESS: [Home], [Home]
   PRESS: [↑]

2. To initiate the BLOCK command:
   PRESS: [Alt]+[F4] (*or* [F12])

3. To highlight the block:
   PRESS: [Enter] *twice*
   The titles in the Doc 1 window should be highlighted.

4. To delete the block:
   PRESS: [Delete]

5. WordPerfect should be displaying the text "Delete Block (Y/N)?:"
   CHOOSE: Yes
   The titles should have been deleted.

6. Center and boldface the following headings at the top of the data in the Doc 1 window:
   TYPE: The Computer Deal
   TYPE: 1st Quarter Sales Data
   The screen should look like Figure 3.7.

Figure 3.7

New titles were inserted and then centered in the Doc 1 window.

```
                        The Computer Deal
                     1st Quarter Sales Data

January
4 computer systems
17 high-resolution color monitors
8 laser printers
3 keyboards
9 mouse

February
4 computer systems
10 high-resolution color monitors
8 laser printers
3 keyboards
9 mouse
4 mouse pads

March
8 computer systems
12 high-resolution color monitors
8 laser printers
3 keyboards                              Doc 1 Pg 1 Ln 1.33" Pos 1"
```

7. Save the data in the Doc 1 window onto the Advantage Diskette as 1STQTR.

Quick Reference
Deleting a Block

1. To initiate the BLOCK command:
   PRESS: [Alt]+[F4] (or [F12])
2. Highlight the block you want to delete.
3. To delete the block:
   PRESS: [Delete]

SAVING A BLOCK

By highlighting a block of text and then using the SAVE command ([F10]), you can give a name to a block of text and then save it onto the disk. Using this procedure you can save text that you might want to retrieve regularly and insert in your documents.

In this section you will use the BLOCK command to save the 4th quarter data (located in the Doc 2 window) onto the Advantage Diskette as 4THQTR.

Perform the following steps:

1. The cursor should be in the Doc 2 window. Position the cursor beneath the "O" of "October."

2. To initiate the BLOCK command and then highlight the block:
    PRESS: Alt + F4 (or F12)
    PRESS: Home, Home
    PRESS: ↓

3. To save the block:
    PRESS: F10

4. WordPerfect is now prompting you to type in a filename for the block (Figure 3.8).

Figure 3.8

Saving a block

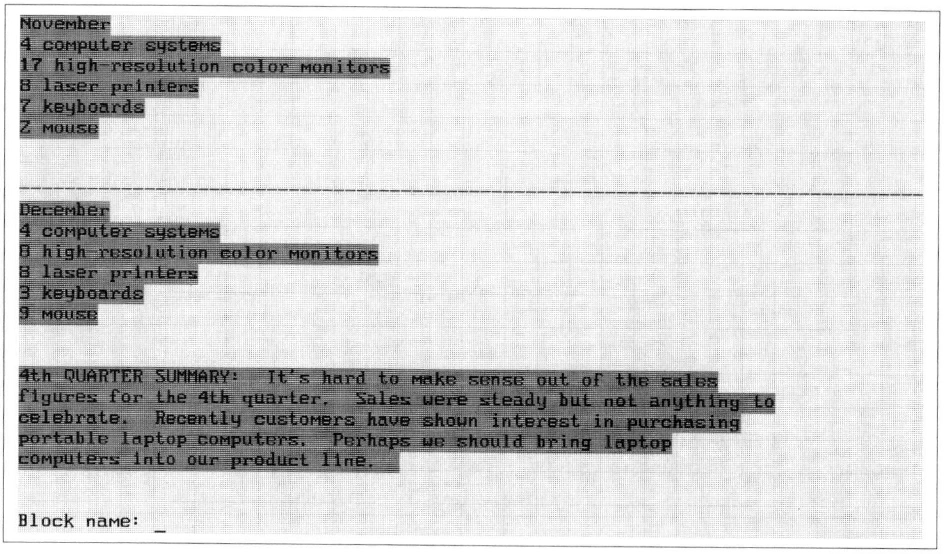

```
November
4 computer systems
17 high-resolution color monitors
8 laser printers
7 keyboards
2 mouse


_____

December
4 computer systems
8 high-resolution color monitors
8 laser printers
3 keyboards
9 mouse


4th QUARTER SUMMARY:   It's hard to make sense out of the sales
figures for the 4th quarter.  Sales were steady but not anything to
celebrate.  Recently customers have shown interest in purchasing
portable laptop computers.  Perhaps we should bring laptop
computers into our product line.

Block name: _
```

a. The Advantage Diskette should be in drive A:.
b. TYPE: A:WPEDIT
c. PRESS: Enter

5. To see that the file WPEDIT was saved, use the LIST FILES command (covered in Session 1) to list the contents of your Advantage Diskette.
   a. PRESS: [F5]
   b. TYPE: A:
   c. PRESS: [Enter]
   One of the files listed should be WPEDIT.

6. To exit the List Files screen:
   PRESS: [F7]

7. Exit the Doc 2 window without saving:
   PRESS: [F7]
   CHOOSE: <u>N</u>o, <u>Y</u>es
   The cursor should be positioned in the Doc 1 window.

Quick Reference
Saving a Block

1. To initiate the BLOCK command:
   PRESS: [Alt]+[F4] (or [F12])
2. Highlight the block that you want to save.
3. To save the block:
   PRESS: [F10]
4. Type in the disk drive designation and name for the block that you want to save (for example: A:FILENAME).
5. To save the file:
   PRESS: [Enter]

SEARCHING FOR ([F2]) AND REPLACING ([Alt]+[F2]) TEXT

The **SEARCH** command ([F2]) provides a time-saving method for moving the cursor to a particular location in a document. The Search option finds the text you're searching for and moves the cursor directly to the right of the first occurrence.

What if you want to replace one word with another word throughout a document? For example, in the WPBLOCK.3 document, the name "WordPerfect" is used many times. What if you wanted to modify this letter so that it describes the WordStar word processing program? It would save time to be able to replace *all* occurrences of "WordPerfect" with "WordStar" with only one command operation. This can be done with the **REPLACE** command ([Alt]+[F2]).

SEARCHING FOR TEXT

In this section you will first use F2 to search for the name "WordPerfect." *Using the menu bar, choose Forward from the Search menu.*

Perform the following steps to search for the name "WordPerfect:"

1. To clear the Doc 1 window so you can retrieve another document:
    PRESS: F7
    CHOOSE: No, No

2. The cursor should be in the Doc 1 window. Retrieve WPBLOCK.3 from the Advantage Diskette.

3. Position the cursor at the beginning of the file.
    PRESS: Home, Home
    PRESS: ↑

4. To initiate the SEARCH command:
    PRESS: F2

5. The text "→Srch:" should be displaying on the bottom of the screen.
    TYPE: WordPerfect
    PRESS: F2

6. The cursor should be positioned after the name "WordPerfect." To get the cursor to jump to the next occurrence of "WordPerfect":
    PRESS: F2 *twice*
    Continue until the text "* Not found *" appears on the bottom of the screen.

Quick Reference
SEARCH Command
F2

1. Position the cursor at the beginning of the document:
    PRESS: Home, Home
    PRESS: ↑
2. To initiate the SEARCH command:
    PRESS: F2
3. TYPE: *the text you want to search for*
4. To begin the search:
    PRESS: F2
5. To search for the next occurrence:
    PRESS: F2 *twice*

REPLACING TEXT

In this section you will use the REPLACE command to search for "WordPerfect" in the WPBLOCK.3 document and replace it with "WordStar." *Using the menu bar, choose Replace from the Search menu.*

When you initiate the REPLACE command, WordPerfect will display the text "w/Confirm? (Y/N)". If you type "N," WordPerfect will proceed through your document and automatically replace text according to your specifications without querying you when it encounters words to be replaced. Otherwise (Y) it will ask if you are sure you want to replace text each time it encounters a word to be replaced.

CAUTION: When searching for and replacing a complete word, you may want to type a space before and after the word you're searching for and the replacement word. Otherwise, you may have some unwanted results. For example, pretend you want to replace all occurrences of the name Donald in your document with Fred. If you don't include spaces, McDonald will have become McFred when you're done using the REPLACE command.

To search for and replace the name "WordPerfect" with the name "WordStar":

1. Position the cursor at the beginning of the file:
   PRESS: (Home), (Home)
   PRESS: (↑)

2. To initiate the REPLACE command:
   PRESS: (Alt)+(F2)

3. To specify that you want to confirm each replace operation:
   CHOOSE: Yes

4. The text "→Srch:" should be displaying on the bottom of the screen.
   TYPE: WordPerfect
   PRESS: (Alt)+(F2)

5. "Replace with:" should be displaying on the bottom of the screen.
   TYPE: WordStar
   PRESS: (Alt)+(F2)

6. The cursor should be positioned beneath the name "WordPerfect." The text "Confirm (Y/N)" should be displaying on the bottom of the screen (Figure 3.9).
   TYPE: Y

Figure 3.9

When using the REPLACE command, if you choose Y when WordPerfect displays the prompt "Confirm (Y/N)," WordPerfect will ask if you are sure you want to replace text every time it encounters a word to be replaced.

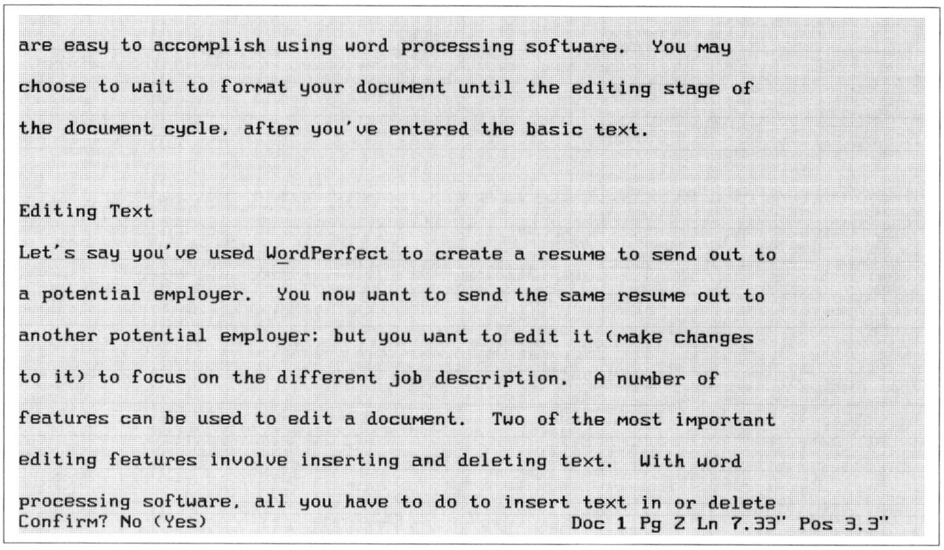

```
are easy to accomplish using word processing software.  You may

choose to wait to format your document until the editing stage of

the document cycle, after you've entered the basic text.


Editing Text

Let's say you've used WordPerfect to create a resume to send out to

a potential employer.  You now want to send the same resume out to

another potential employer; but you want to edit it (make changes

to it) to focus on the different job description.  A number of

features can be used to edit a document.  Two of the most important

editing features involve inserting and deleting text.  With word

processing software, all you have to do to insert text in or delete
Confirm? No (Yes)                                Doc 1 Pg 2 Ln 7.33" Pos 3.3"
```

7. Continue pressing "Y" until all occurrences of the name "WordPerfect" have been replaced with "WordStar."

8. Save WPBLOCK.3 onto the Advantage Diskette, and then use [F7] to clear the WPBLOCK.3 document from the Doc1 window.

Quick Reference
Replace
Command
[Alt]+[F2]

1. Position the cursor at the beginning of the document:
   PRESS: [Home], [Home]
   PRESS: [↑]
2. To initiate the REPLACE command:
   PRESS: [Alt]+[F2]
3. TYPE: *the text you want to search for*
   PRESS: [Alt]+[F2]
4. TYPE: *the text you want to replace the old text with*
   PRESS: [Alt]+[F2]
5. Type Y or N, depending on whether you want WordPerfect to prompt you each time to confirm the replacement.
6. If you typed Y in the previous step, continue typing Y until all replacements have been made.

SPELL-CHECKING A DOCUMENT (Ctrl+F2)

In this section you will use the SPELL command (Ctrl+F2) to check the spelling of a file called WPSPELL that is stored on the Advantage Diskette. *Using the menu bar, choose Speller from the Menu.*

When you check a document for spelling, you have the following options:

- **Skip Once.** If the spelling checker highlights a word that is spelled correctly, you can tell WordPerfect to skip it and continue spell-checking the document.

- **Skip.** This option is the same as the Skip Once option except that it skips the word throughout the document.

- **Add.** If you use a word frequently that isn't in the WordPerfect spell-checking dictionary, you can add it to the dictionary with this option. The next time you spell-check a document, WordPerfect won't flag the word as misspelled.

- **Edit.** If WordPerfect doesn't provide you with the correct spelling for a highlighted word, use this option to edit the word. When you are finished editing the word, press F7 to continue spell-checking.

- **Look Up.** This option enables you to search for a word in the dictionary that matches a certain pattern. Based on this pattern, the correct spelling may list on the screen. This option is useful if WordPerfect doesn't provide you with suggested correct spellings for a given word.

- **Ignore Numbers.** When this option is chosen, the speller won't consider words that contain numbers to be misspelled. (*Note:* Use this option with caution. If you accidentally typed a number in a word, the speller will ignore the mistake.)

- **Double Word.** The speller has discovered a double word occurrence (accidental repetition), and gives you the option of deleting the second word, skipping it, or editing it.

To spell-check the WPSPELL document, perform the following steps:

1. Retrieve the WPSPELL document from the Advantage Diskette.

2. To initiate the SPELL command:
    PRESS: Ctrl+F2

3. To spell-check the document:
   CHOOSE: Document

4. As shown in Figure 3.10, "hav" should be highlighted. A list of correct spellings should be listed below.
   TYPE: *the letter that corresponds to the correct spelling (have)*

Figure 3.10

The Spelling Checker (Ctrl + F2). The misspelled word "hav" is highlighted. A list of correct spellings is displaying on the bottom of the screen.

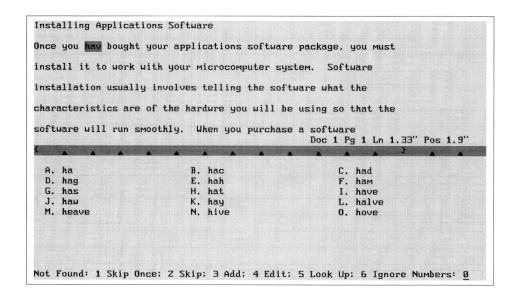

```
Installing Applications Software

Once you hav bought your applications software package, you must

install it to work with your microcomputer system.  Software

installation usually involves telling the software what the

characteristics are of the hardwre you will be using so that the

software will run smoothly.  When you purchase a software
                                       Doc 1 Pg 1 Ln 1.33" Pos 1.9"

     A. ha            B. hac            C. had
     D. hag           E. hah            F. ham
     G. has           H. hat            I. have
     J. haw           K. hay            L. halve
     M. heave         N. hive           O. hove



Not Found: 1 Skip Once; 2 Skip; 3 Add; 4 Edit; 5 Look Up; 6 Ignore Numbers: 0
```

5. "hardwre" should now be highlighted.
   TYPE: *the letter that corresponds to the correct spelling (hardware)*

6. "progrm" should now be highlighted.
   TYPE: *the letter that corresponds to the correct spelling (program)*

7. Continue in this manner until you have finished spell-checking the document. WordPerfect will instruct you to press any key.

8. Save the document onto the Advantage Diskette as WPSPELL.

Quick Reference
SPELL Command
Ctrl+F2

1. To initiate the SPELL command:
   PRESS: Ctrl+F2
2. Specify whether you want to spell-check a (1) Word, (2) Page, or (3) Document.
3. When the speller highlights a word, choose an option to (1) Skip Once, (2) Skip, (3) Add, (4) Edit, (5) Look Up, or (6) Ignore Numbers.

THESAURUS (Alt+F1)

What if you can't think of the right word to use in a sentence? The **THESAURUS** command (Alt+F1) can provide you with a list of words that have similar meaning. *Using the menu bar, choose Thesaurus from the Tools menu.* To illustrate:

1. The WPSPELL document should be stored in the Doc 1 window.

2. Position the cursor beneath the word "package" in the first sentence.

3. To initiate the THESAURUS command:
    PRESS: Alt+F1
    The screen should look similar to Figure 3.11.

Figure 3.11

The Thesaurus (Alt+F1). The word "package" is highlighted and a list of words with similar meaning is displaying below.

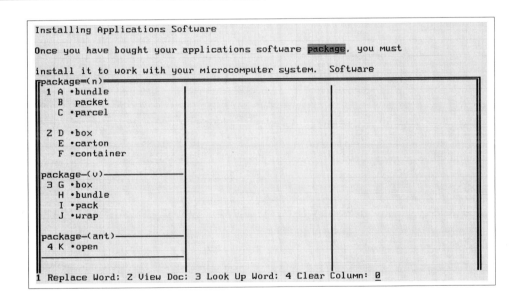

```
Installing Applications Software

Once you have bought your applications software package, you must

install it to work with your microcomputer system. Software
package=(n)
    1 A •bundle
      B  packet
      C •parcel

    2 D •box
      E •carton
      F •container

package—(v)
    3 G •box
      H •bundle
      I •pack
      J •wrap

package—(ant)
    4 K •open


1 Replace Word; 2 View Doc; 3 Look Up Word; 4 Clear Column: 0
```

4. To substitute the word "packet" for "package," choose the Replace Word option:
    CHOOSE: 1
    TYPE: B
    The document should be displaying on the screen again, with "packet" in place of "package."

Using the THESAURUS command, the View Doc option enables you to view more of your document on the screen without leaving the THESAURUS command. The Look Up Word option enables you to type in a word directly to be looked up in the thesaurus. The Clear Column option enables you clear the last column of words displayed on the screen.

5. Experiment using the THESAURUS command. When you are through, exit the document without saving using the EXIT command:
PRESS: [F7]
CHOOSE: <u>No</u>, <u>No</u>

Quick Reference
Thesaurus
[Alt]+[F1]

1. Position the cursor on a word you want to look up.
2. To initiate the THESAURUS command:
   PRESS: [Alt]+[F1]
3. Choose an option to either (1) Replace Word, (2) View Document, (3) Look Up Word, or (4) Clear Column.

SUMMARY

In this session, you practiced working with more than one document at a time. Specifically, you learned how to display two windows on the screen at once and to copy text from the Doc 1 window into the Doc 2 window.

Searching for text using [F2] is useful if you want to move the cursor to a certain location in your document quickly or if you want to see if you included specific text in your document. Replacing text using [Alt]+[F2] can save you valuable editing time if you need to search for specific characters and then replace them with different characters.

The session concluded with the SPELL command ([Ctrl]+[F2]) and the Thesaurus command ([Alt]+[F1]).

The commands described in this session are frequently used for editing documents.

COMMAND SUMMARY

The table on the next page provides a list of the commands and procedures covered in this session.

Table 3.1	Shift+F3	Switch into the Doc 2 window
Command Summary	Ctrl+F3, Window, type # of lines for window size, Enter	Change the size of the current window
	Ctrl+F4, choose an option, Copy, move cursor, Enter	Copy a sentence, paragraph, or page
	Ctrl+F4, choose an option, Move, move cursor, Enter	Move a sentence, paragraph, or page
	Ctrl+F4, choose an option, Delete	Delete a sentence, paragraph, or page
	F1	Use this key to restore previously deleted text
	Alt+F4, highlight block, Ctrl+F4, Block, choose Move or Copy, move cursor, Enter	Move or copy a block
	Alt+F4, highlight block, Delete	Delete a block
	Alt+F4, highlight block, F10, type a disk drive and filename, Enter	Save a block
	F2, type text to be searched for, F2	Search for text
	Alt+F2, type search text, Alt+F2, type replacement text, Alt+F2	Search for and then replace text
	Ctrl+F2	Spell-check
	Alt+F1	Thesaurus

KEY TERMS

Move (Ctrl+F4)   In WordPerfect, this command is used to move, to copy, and to delete sentences, paragraphs, and pages.

Search (F2) and Replace (Alt+F2)   In WordPerfect, these commands enable you to search for text, or to search for and then replace text in a document.

Spell (Ctrl+F2)   A WordPerfect command used to check documents for spelling errors; the spelling checker will display a list of correct spellings.

Switch (Shift+F3)   In WordPerfect, this command moves the cursor into the Doc 2 window from the Doc 1 window, and vice versa.

Thesaurus (Alt+F1)   A WordPerfect command that enables the user to display on the screen a list of words that have similar meaning to the word the cursor is highlighting.

Window (Ctrl+F3)   In WordPerfect, this command enables you to display two documents on the screen at once by changing the number of lines that are displayed in each window.

EXERCISES

SHORT ANSWER

1. What capabilities does the THESAURUS command provide?
2. When might you want to use the WINDOW command?
3. When you work with documents stored in the Doc 1 and Doc 2 windows, are the two documents independent of each other?
4. During a SPELL operation, for what would you use the Add option?
5. Describe the procedure used to copy from one document window to another.
6. During a SPELL operation, for what would you use the Skip option?
7. When you are using the MOVE command to copy or highlight text, what must you do after highlighting the text you want to move or copy?
8. Why is it sometimes useful to use both the Doc 1 and Doc 2 windows?
9. When you are copying, moving, or deleting text, why is it sometimes necessary to use the BLOCK command rather than the MOVE command?
10. When replacing a word in a document, why should you include a space before and after the word you're searching for and the word you're replacing with?

HANDS-ON

1. To practice using the SPELL and THESAURUS commands, perform the following steps:
   a. Retrieve BADMEMO from the Advantage Diskette.
   b. Use the SPELL command to correct any spelling mistakes.

     c. Use the THESAURUS command to find different words for:
- "available" in the first paragraph.
- "previously" in the first paragraph.

     d. Save the document as GOODMEMO onto the Advantage Diskette.

2. To practice using block operations, retrieve HARDWARE from the Advantage Diskette and then perform the following steps:
   a. Move the second paragraph to follow the third paragraph.
   b. Copy the first paragraph into the Doc 2 window.
   c. Switch into the Doc 1 window.
   d. Change the third paragraph to uppercase.
   e. Underline and boldface the third paragraph.
   f. Save the third paragraph onto the Advantage Diskette as BLOCK1.3.
   g. Switch into the Doc 2 window. Using some of the procedures you learned in Session 2, perform the following blocking tasks:
      (1) Underline the first sentence.
      (2) Boldface the second sentence.
      (3) Change the case of the first sentence to uppercase.
      (4) Save this paragraph onto the Advantage Diskette as BLOCK2.3 and then print it.
      (5) Exit the Doc 2 window.
   h. Print BLOCK1.3.

3. In this exercise, you will use the SEARCH and REPLACE commands. Clear the data out of the Doc 1 window without saving. Retrieve WPSPELL.3 from the Advantage Diskette and then perform the following tasks:
   a. Search for the characters "PC" to replace.
   b. Replace all occurrences of the characters "PC" with the word "microcomputer" in the file.
   c. Spell-check the document.

4. In this exercise you will practice using the REPLACE command to edit the MISDEPT document that is stored on the Advantage Diskette. Perform the following steps:
   a. Retrieve MISDEPT from the Advantage Diskette.
   b. Use the REPLACE command to change the name of the department from "Management Information Systems Department" to "Office Automation Division."
   c. Use the REPLACE command to boldface every occurrence of "OS/5 Version 6.0 Batch Release 2.109" in the document.
   d. Save the document as MISDEPT onto the Advantage Diskette and replace the old version.

5. To practice using the BLOCK MOVE command, retrieve the NAMES file from the Advantage Diskette and then perform the following tasks:
   a. Insert your name and address in the list.
   b. Using block commands, rearrange the names so they appear in alphabetical order by last name.

c.   Print the newly ordered list.

d.   Rearrange the names again so they appear in alphabetical order by city.

e.   Print this list.

f.   Exit this document without saving it.

6.   The objective of this exercise is to practice moving and copying document text. Create the following document:

```
Alpha Beta Computer Rentals
5900 Algonquin Road, Suite 775
Asheville, NC 28804


January 15, 1993



Ms. Lolita Balfour
2910 Freemont Road
Raleigh, NC 27610

Dear Ms. Balfour:

Thank you for your order! I am writing to confirm
your order of the following items to be delivered
to your premises on January 29, 1993.
```

Items Shipped

```
MONITOR:       TLC MultipleSync 4GH Monitor
OPTIONS:       2400 Baud Internal Modem
HARD DISK:     MaxStore 512Mb Hard Drive
CPU:           Compact 486/33 with 16Mb RAM
VIDEO CARD:    ABC Ultrasonic Graph Card

Yours Truly,


your name
Accounts Representative

P.S. If I can be of any assistance, please call me
at 999-999-9999.
```

a.   Save the document as ORDERS onto the Advantage Diskette.

b.   Move the text after the "P.S." (starting with the word "If") to above the line "Yours truly." (Leave the "P.S." at the bottom of the letter.)

c.   Move the first sentence in the first paragraph ("Thank you for your order!") to after the "P.S." on the last line of the document.

    d. Change the order of the Items Shipped to the following: CPU, HARD DISK, MONITOR, VIDEO CARD, and OPTIONS.

    e. Copy the company name "Alpha Beta Computer Rentals" from the top of the page to below the title "Accounts Representative."

    f. Save (and replace) ORDERS onto the Advantage Diskette.

    g. Print ORDERS.

SESSION 4

PRINTING AND FILE-MANAGEMENT COMMANDS

Now that you've learned about how to create and edit document files, it's time to learn more about printing. In addition, as you store more and more files on disk, it becomes increasingly important to know how to manage them.

PREVIEW

When you have completed this session, you will be able to:

Prepare a document to be printed using:
Margin commands.
Justification changes.
Widows and orphans.
Page numbering.
Headers and footers.
•
Print multiple copies and control the printer.
•
Include graphics in a document.
•
Use file-management commands.

Why Is This Session Important?
Preparing a Document to Be Printed
      Changing Left and Right Margins
      Changing Top and Bottom Margins
      Changing Justification
      Widows and Orphans
      Page Numbering
      Headers and Footers
Printing (Shift+F7)
      Printing Multiple Pages and Copies
      Controlling the Printer
      Printing a Block
Graphics (Alt+F9)
      Graphics Boxes
      Graphics Box Contents
      Creating a Graphics Box
File Management Commands (F5)
Summary
      Command Summary
Key Terms
Exercises
      Short Answer
      Hands-On

WHY IS THIS SESSION IMPORTANT?

WordPerfect offers a number of ways to enhance the appearance of your printed documents. In this session you learn how to change margins, the justification of a document, protect against widows and orphans (which we describe shortly), include page numbers, include a header or a footer, and include graphics in a document. Using these options improves the appearance of your printed documents and helps to enhance the clarity of your message.

You will also see how to use the List Files ((F5)) options to manage files easily.

Before proceeding, make sure the following are true:

1. You have access to WordPerfect 5.1.

2. Your Advantage Diskette is inserted in the drive. You will save your work onto the diskette and retrieve the files that have been created for you. (Note: The Advantage Diskette can be made by copying all the files off your instructor's Master Advantage Diskette onto a formatted diskette.)

PREPARING A DOCUMENT TO BE PRINTED

The WordPerfect Format menu ((Shift)+(F8)) provides you with options to change how your document will look when printed. (It can be printed without formatting it.) *Using the menu bar, display the Layout menu.*

CAUTION: As with other format commands that we've described (in Session 2), you must position the cursor where you want the command to begin affecting your document. The document is affected from the current cursor position downward. Therefore, if you want a command to affect an entire document, position the cursor at the top of the document before executing the command.

CHANGING LEFT AND RIGHT MARGINS

Unless you issue a command to change the margins, WordPerfect will print your documents with a 1-inch left margin and a 1-inch right margin. Depending on your needs, you may want to change the margins to be either larger or smaller. For example, this guide was printed with a 2-1/2-inch left margin so notes and messages could be placed there. To change the left and right margins, use the FORMAT command ((Shift)+(F8)) and then choose the Line option. *Using the menu bar, select Line from the Layout menu.* Choose Margins, and then type in the new margin specification.

As mentioned earlier, when you change a margin specification, which inserts a code in your document, the document is affected from the current cursor position downward. The new margin setting is in effect until another margin code is encountered in the document. The new margin size must be typed in using tenths of an inch. For example, if you want a margin to be 2-1/2-inches wide, you would type 2.5 for the new margin size.

In this step you will change the left margin of the entire WPBLOCK.3 document from 1 inch to 2 inches. Therefore, before you issue the MARGIN-CHANGE command, you must position the cursor at the top of the document.

1. Retrieve WPBLOCK.3 from the Advantage Diskette.

2. To make sure the cursor is at the top of the document:
    PRESS: [Home], [Home]
    PRESS: [↑]

3. To initiate the FORMAT command in order to change the margins:
    PRESS: [Shift]+[F8]
    CHOOSE: Line
    CHOOSE: Margins

4. WordPerfect is now waiting for you to type in a number corresponding to the new left margin (2 inches).
    TYPE: 2
    PRESS: [Enter]

5. To exit back to your document:
    PRESS: [F7] *twice*

6. At this point the document looks the same. But if you look down on the status line, the position indicator reads 2 (Figure 4.1). To reform the text according to the new margin:
    PRESS: [↓] *twice*

Quick Reference
Changing Margins
[Shift]+[F8]

1. Position the cursor where the margin change should begin taking effect.
2. PRESS: [Shift]+[F8]
3. CHOOSE: Line, Margins
4. TYPE: *a number that corresponds to the new margin width (in inches)*
    PRESS: [Enter]
5. PRESS: [F7] *twice*

Figure 4.1

The left margin
of the entire
WPBLOCK.3
document has
been changed
from 1 inch to
2 inches.

```
Entering Text

After you have loaded your word processing software into RAM, the

next step is to enter, or key in, your text.  When entering text,

you will deal with (1) cursor movement, (2) word wrap and the Enter

key, (3) scrolling, and (4) formatting.

     In most word processing programs, the cursor is a blinking or

highlighted line (or block), about as wide as a character, that

marks where the next character will be entered or the starting

point of the next command operation.  As you type a character, the

cursor moves to the right.  You can control where the cursor is

positioned in order to edit text by using the cursor-movement keys

on your keyboard.

C:\IRWIN\DISKETTE\WPBLOCK.3                        Doc 1 Pg 1 Ln 1" Pos 2"
```

7. To position the cursor at the top of the document and then see the margin-change code that WordPerfect inserted in your document, use the REVEAL CODES command (the REVEAL CODES command was described in Session 1):
PRESS: (Home), (Home)
PRESS: (↑)
PRESS: (Alt)+(F3) (or (F11))
The screen should look similar to Figure 4.2. L/R Mar:2",1" means that the left margin is 2 inches wide and the right margin is 1 inch wide. Any text you type at this point will adhere to these margin settings unless you either delete the margin-change code using the Reveal Codes screen or insert another margin-change code below.

If you decide later that you don't want the margins to be changed, you can delete the code. To illustrate the process, in the following step you will delete the margin-change code.

8. The cursor should still be positioned to the right of the margin-change code on the Reveal Codes screen. To delete this code:
PRESS: (BackSpace)
The left margin is now 1 inch.

9. To return to the document by turning the REVEAL CODES command off:
PRESS: (Alt)+(F3) (or (F11))

Figure 4.2

Revealing
codes. The
margin-change
code has been
inserted at the
top of the
document.

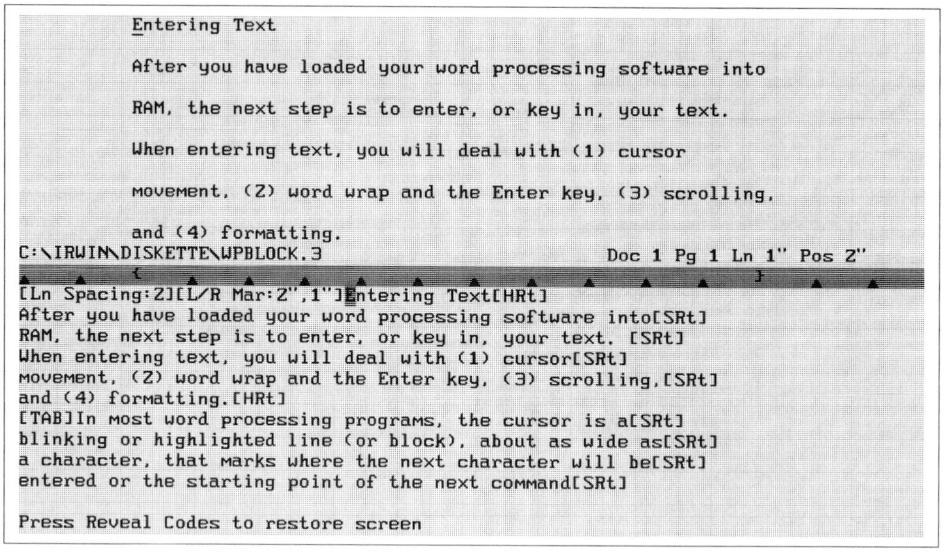

```
        Entering Text

        After you have loaded your word processing software into

        RAM, the next step is to enter, or key in, your text.

        When entering text, you will deal with (1) cursor

        movement, (2) word wrap and the Enter key, (3) scrolling,

        and (4) formatting.
C:\IRWIN\DISKETTE\WPBLOCK.3                          Doc 1 Pg 1 Ln 1" Pos 2"
    ▲    {        ▲        ▲      ▲       ▲      ▲    }    ▲      ▲
[Ln Spacing:2][L/R Mar:2",1"]Entering Text[HRt]
After you have loaded your word processing software into[SRt]
RAM, the next step is to enter, or key in, your text. [SRt]
When entering text, you will deal with (1) cursor[SRt]
movement, (2) word wrap and the Enter key, (3) scrolling,[SRt]
and (4) formatting.[HRt]
[TAB]In most word processing programs, the cursor is a[SRt]
blinking or highlighted line (or block), about as wide as[SRt]
a character, that marks where the next character will be[SRt]
entered or the starting point of the next command[SRt]

Press Reveal Codes to restore screen
```

Quick Reference
Deleting a Code

1. To reveal codes:
   PRESS: [Alt]+[F3] (*or* [F11])
2. Position the cursor to the right of the code and then press [BackSpace] to delete the unwanted code. If you position the cursor on the code, press [Delete] to delete the code.

CHANGING TOP AND BOTTOM MARGINS

Unless you issue a command to change the margins, WordPerfect will print your documents with a 1-inch top margin and a 1-inch bottom margin. Users often change the top or bottom margin to 1/2-inch (or .5) when they include page numbers in their documents (you learn how to include page numbers shortly.) Otherwise, the page number prints too far from the edge of the page.

To change the top and/or bottom margin, use the FORMAT command ([Shift]+[F8]) and then choose the Page option. Figure 4.3 displays the Page Format menu. *Using the menu bar, select Page from the Layout menu.* Choose Margins, and then type in the new margin specification in tenths of an inch. When finished, press [F7] to return to your document.

Figure 4.3

The Page
Format
menu

```
Format: Page

    1 - Center Page (top to bottom)    No

    2 - Force Odd/Even Page

    3 - Headers

    4 - Footers

    5 - Margins - Top                  1"
                  Bottom               1"

    6 - Page Numbering

    7 - Paper Size                     8.5" x 11"
                  Type                 Standard

    8 - Suppress (this page only)




Selection: 0
```

CHANGING JUSTIFICATION

By changing the **justification** of your document, you can change the way text is aligned along the margins of the printed page. On the screen, your documents always appear left-justified (evenly aligned on the left with the text ragged on the right). But when printed, your documents always appear fully-justified (with the text on both sides aligned evenly with the margins) unless you use the FORMAT command to change this default assumption. In some documents you might not want the uneven word spaces that allow even alignment on both sides, so you would justify the left side only.

To illustrate:

1. Make sure the Advantage Diskette is in drive A:.

2. If WPBLOCK.4 isn't already displaying on the screen, retrieve it from the Advantage Diskette.

3. Note that, on the screen, the right margin appears ragged.

4. Using the following procedure, view the first page of this document on the screen so you can see how it will appear when it is printed:
    PRESS: Shift+F7
    CHOOSE: View Document
    Note that the page appears evenly aligned on both sides of the text.
    To exit to the document screen:
    PRESS: F7

The following procedure leads you through changing the justification of the WPBLOCK.4 document so that the right margin appears ragged when printed.

1. To position the cursor at the top of the document:
   PRESS: [Home], [Home]
   PRESS: [↑]

2. To initiate the FORMAT command:
   PRESS: [Shift]+[F8]

3. CHOOSE: Line, Justification
   The screen should look like Figure 4.4.

Figure 4.4

The Justification menu

```
Format: Line

    1 - Hyphenation                          No

    2 - Hyphenation Zone - Left              10%
                           Right             4%

    3 - Justification                        Full

    4 - Line Height                          Auto

    5 - Line Numbering                       No

    6 - Line Spacing                         2

    7 - Margins - Left                       1"
                  Right                      1"

    8 - Tab Set                              Rel: -1", every 0.5"

    9 - Widow/Orphan Protection              No


Justification: 1 Left; 2 Center; 3 Right; 4 Full: 0
```

4. To tell WordPerfect that you want the document to appear evenly aligned on the left margin only:
   CHOOSE: Left

5. To exit this menu:
   PRESS: [F7]

6. To view the first page of your document:
   PRESS: [Shift]+[F7]
   CHOOSE: View Document
   Note that the printed page doesn't appear evenly aligned along the right margin (Figure 4.5).

Figure 4.5

WPBLOCK.3
is now left-
justified.

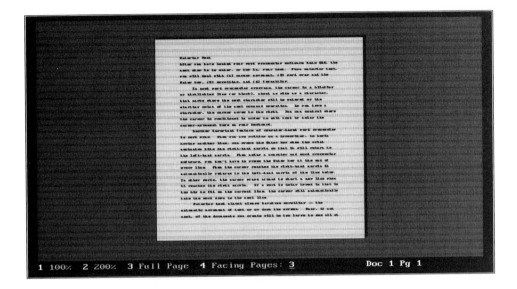

7. To exit back to your document:
   PRESS: F7

8. To see the code that WordPerfect embedded in your document:
   PRESS: Alt+F3 (*or* F11)
   The [Just:Left] code should be displaying in your document.

9. To exit the Reveal Codes screen:
   PRESS: Alt+F3 (*or* F11)
   If you want the document to appear evenly aligned along the right margin,
   simply delete the justification code from the Reveal Codes screen.

Quick Reference
Changing
Justification

1. Position the cursor where the Justification option should begin taking effect.
2. To initiate the FORMAT command:
   PRESS: Shift+F8
3. CHOOSE: Line, Justification
4. Choose the option you want.
5. To exit this menu:
   PRESS: F7

WIDOWS AND ORPHANS

WordPerfect provides a command that enables you to protect against widows and orphans in multipage documents; many users use this command with all their documents. A **widow** is created when a paragraph ends on the first line of a page (a widow exists on page 5 of the WPBLOCK.4 document). An **orphan** is created when a paragraph begins on the last line of a page. Ideally, a document shouldn't contain any widows or orphans. The procedure to protect against widows and orphans uses the FORMAT command. To protect the entire WPBLOCK document, perform the following procedure:

1. To clear the screen so you can work with another document:
   PRESS: F7
   CHOOSE: No, No

2. Retrieve WPBLOCK.4 from the Advantage Diskette.

3. The WPBLOCK.4 document should be displaying on the screen. Position the cursor at the top of the document:
   PRESS: Home, Home
   PRESS: ↑

4. To first view the widow on page 5 of the WPBLOCK document:
   PRESS: PgDn *four times*
   PRESS: ↑
   The screen should look like Figure 4.6. In the next few steps you will protect against widows and orphans.

Figure 4.6

A widow is
displaying in the
WPBLOCK.4
document.

```
the appropriate words.  This feature is useful when you know what

you want to say but can't find the right words.


Printing

Once you've created a document and you're pleased with it, you'll

probably want to print the document out on a printer.  Printing a

document involves connecting your printer to your computer, turning

the printer on, and then issuing the command to print your

document.  However, before you actually print your document, you

may want to enhance the final appearance of the printed page --

that is to change the formatting.

    For example, you may want to change the justification of your
C:\IRWIN\ADV-FILE\WPBLOCK.4                    Doc 1 Pg 4 Ln 9.67" Pos 1"
```

5. To position the cursor at the top of the document:
   PRESS: Home, Home
   PRESS: ↑

6. To initiate the FORMAT command:
   PRESS: [Shift]+[F8]

7. CHOOSE: Line
   CHOOSE: Widow/Orphan Protection

8. To turn protection on:
   CHOOSE: Yes

9. To exit the Format menu:
   PRESS: [F7]

10. To see if the widow still exists on page 5:
    PRESS: [PgDn] *four times*
    Note that the widow is gone; WordPerfect automatically moved the last line from the previous page to the top of page 5.

Quick Reference
Protecting Against Widows/Orphans

1. Position the cursor where the WIDOW/ORPHAN command should begin taking effect.
2. To initiate the FORMAT command:
   PRESS: [Shift]+[F8]
3. CHOOSE: Line, Widow/Orphan Protection
4. To turn protection on, type Y. To turn protection off, type N.
5. To exit the Format menu:
   PRESS: [F7]

PAGE NUMBERING

WordPerfect will number the pages in your documents only if you instruct it to using the PAGE NUMBERING command or the HEADERS or FOOTERS command. (Headers and footers are described in the next section.) Page numbers appear in your documents only when they are printed.

As with other formatting commands, page numbers will be inserted in your document beginning with the page in which the code is initially entered. To insert a page number, use the FORMAT command ([Shift]+[F8]) and then choose the Page option. *Using the menu bar, choose Page from the Layout menu.* Next you must choose the Page Numbering option and then specify the page number position. (Other page numbering options are available which we describe shortly.)

In the steps below, we lead you through printing the WPBLOCK document with page numbers.

1. Retrieve WPBLOCK.4 from the Advantage Diskette.

2. To position the cursor at the top of the document:
   PRESS: [Home], [Home]
   PRESS: [↑]

3. To initiate the FORMAT command:
   PRESS: [Shift]+[F8]

4. CHOOSE: Page, Page Numbering
   CHOOSE: Page Number Position
   The screen should look like Figure 4.7. WordPerfect gives you eight different choices for positioning the page numbers.

Figure 4.7

The Page Number Position menu. The numbers on the pages represent page number positions. If, for example, you want to print page numbers in alternating positions on the bottom of every page, you would choose option 8.

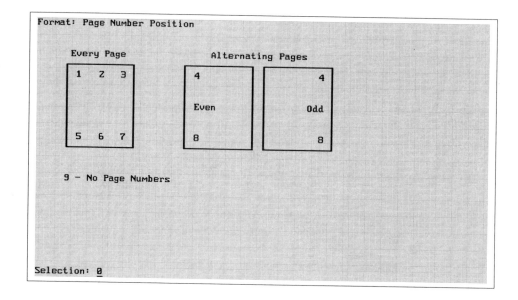

```
Format: Page Number Position


    Every Page                  Alternating Pages

    ┌───────────┐        ┌───────────┐  ┌───────────┐
    │ 1   2   3 │        │ 4         │  │         4 │
    │           │        │           │  │           │
    │           │        │  Even     │  │     Odd   │
    │           │        │           │  │           │
    │ 5   6   7 │        │ 8         │  │         8 │
    └───────────┘        └───────────┘  └───────────┘

    9 - No Page Numbers




Selection: 0
```

---

5. To print a page number in the bottom-center of every page:
   CHOOSE: 6

6. To exit the Format menu:
   PRESS: [F7]

7. To print the entire WPBLOCK document with newly added page numbers:
   PRESS: [Shift]+[F7]
   CHOOSE: Full Document

CAUTION: The page number code can be positioned after other codes on the current page, but *not* after spaces or characters if you want the page number to print on the page in which the code has been entered. The page number will print on subsequent pages, however.

CAUTION: When page numbers are included on the bottom of the page, you may want to make the bottom margin smaller. Otherwise too much space appears between the page number and the edge of the paper. Likewise, when page numbers appear at the top of the page you may want to make the top margin smaller.

....

Quick Reference
Page Numbering

1. To initiate the FORMAT command:
   PRESS: Shift+F8
2. CHOOSE: Page, Page Numbering
3. CHOOSE: Page Number Position
4. Type a number that corresponds to where you want the page number positioned on the page when your document is printed.
5. To exit the Format menu:
   PRESS: F7

....

NEW PAGE NUMBER

After choosing the PAGE NUMBERING command from the Page menu, WordPerfect displays the menu pictured in Figure 4.8. This section describes how you might use the New Page Number option.

Figure 4.8

The Page Numbering Format menu

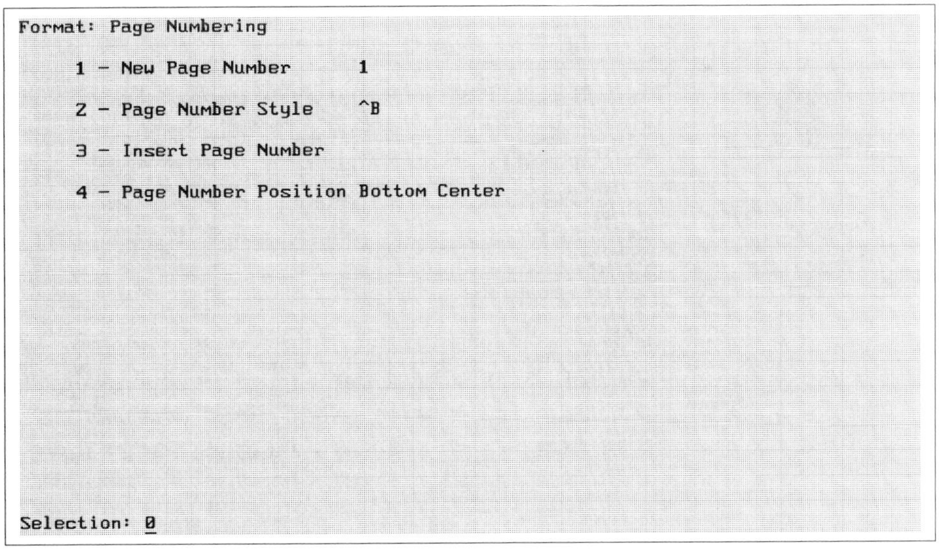

```
Format: Page Numbering

    1 - New Page Number        1

    2 - Page Number Style      ^B

    3 - Insert Page Number

    4 - Page Number Position   Bottom Center




Selection: 0
```

WordPerfect knows the physical page number of every page in your document and prints the physical page number unless you use the **NEW PAGE NUMBER** command to specify otherwise. In other words, without any special instructions, WordPerfect will print the number 2 on the bottom of page 2.

In some cases, you don't want the physical page number to print. For example, you might want page numbering to begin with the number 1 on page 2 since page 1 is a title page. Another good application for the NEW PAGE NUMBER command is when you have a large document that has been separated into two or more files. If the first document is 26 pages, you will want the first page of the second document to begin numbering with 27.

If you want the page numbers to display as roman numerals, type the new page number as a roman numeral (for example, i, ii, iii, iv, and so on). Roman numerals are often used to number the pages in the frontmatter of a report or book.

PAGE NUMBER STYLE

The **PAGE NUMBER STYLE** command (shown in Figure 4.8) can be used to customize the way the page number appears on the page. The code that WordPerfect uses to represent the page number is ^B (^ represents pressing `Ctrl`). Unless you use the PAGE NUMBER STYLE command, WordPerfect will print plain page numbers (1, 2, 3, and so on), as represented by ^B. If you want the page number to print as Page 1, Page 2, Page 3, and so on, type `Page ^B` after choosing the PAGE NUMBER STYLE command. Or if you are printing a 12-page document, type `^B of 12` after choosing the PAGE NUMBER STYLE command.

HEADERS AND FOOTERS

As we described in Session 1, a **header** is information that appears on the top of every page when your document is printed. Textbooks often include the chapter title in the header (called a "runninghead") for each page. A **footer** (or "runningfoot") is information that appears on the bottom of every page when your document is printed. When adding a header or a footer to a document, position the cursor at the top of the page on which you want the header or footer to first appear.

If ^B (^ represents pressing `Ctrl`) is inserted in the header or footer, when the document is printed the current page number will appear. If you know your document is 12 pages long when printed, you may want to include the following footer: ^B of 12. Or you may want to include the following header: Page ^B. Or: — ^B —.

In this section you will add a header that includes the current date to the WPBLOCK document. Because the header will print on every page, you must first position the cursor at the beginning of the document. Perform the following steps:

1.   Retrieve WPBLOCK.4 from the Advantage Diskette (if you haven't already).

2. To position the cursor at the top of the document:
    PRESS: [Home], [Home]
    PRESS: [↑]

3. To initiate the FORMAT command:
    PRESS: [Shift]+[F8]

4. CHOOSE: Page, Header

5. At the bottom of the screen you have the choice of Header A or Header B.
    WordPerfect enables you to include different headers on alternate pages. Since
    you're only including one header, it doesn't matter which option you choose.
    CHOOSE: Header A

6. Additional options should be displaying on the bottom of the screen (Figure
    4.9). To tell WordPerfect you want the header to print on every page:

Figure 4.9

Header/Footer
options

```
Format: Page

    1 - Center Page (top to bottom)     No

    2 - Force Odd/Even Page

    3 - Headers

    4 - Footers

    5 - Margins - Top                   1"
                  Bottom                1"

    6 - Page Numbering

    7 - Paper Size                      8.5" x 11"
              Type                      Standard

    8 - Suppress (this page only)



1 Discontinue: 2 Every Page: 3 Odd Pages: 4 Even Pages: 5 Edit: 0
```

CHOOSE: Every Page

7. The screen should have cleared. WordPerfect is waiting for you to type header
    text into the document. To insert the current date (the DATE command was
    described in Session 2):
    PRESS: [Shift]+[F5]
    CHOOSE: Date Text
    The screen should look similar to Figure 4.10, but showing the current date.

Figure 4.10

Including the
current date
in a header

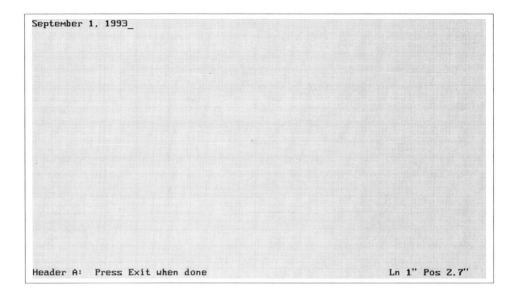

8. To exit to your document:
    PRESS: F7 *twice*

9. To print the WPBLOCK document with the new header information:
    PRESS: Shift+F7
    CHOOSE: Full Document

CAUTION: The header/footer code can be positioned after other codes on the current page, but *not* after spaces or characters if you want the header/footer to print on the page in which the code has been entered. The header/footer will print on subsequent pages, however.

CAUTION: When footers are included in a document, you may want to make the bottom margin smaller. Otherwise too much space appears between the footer and the bottom of the paper. Likewise, when headers are included in a document, you may want to make the top margin smaller.

PRINTING (Shift+F7)

In this section, we describe some of the different options available when you print a document. Figure 4.11 shows the menu that displays after using the PRINT command (Shift+F7). *Using the menu bar, choose Print from the File menu.*

Quick Reference
Headers and Footers

1. To initiate the FORMAT command:
   PRESS: Shift+F8
2. CHOOSE: Page
3. CHOOSE: Header *or* Footer
4. Choose (1) Header A, (2) Header B, (3) Footer A, or (4) Footer B.
5. Choose an option that corresponds to when you want the header/footer to be printed.
6. TYPE: *the information you want to appear in the header or footer*
7. To exit to your document:
   PRESS: F7 *twice*

Quick Reference
Including Page Numbers in the Header/Footer

Perform the steps to create a header/footer. When typing in the text for the header/footer, type `^B` if you want the current page number to print.

Figure 4.11

The Print menu

```
Print

     1 - Full Document
     2 - Page
     3 - Document on Disk
     4 - Control Printer
     5 - Multiple Pages
     6 - View Document
     7 - Initialize Printer

Options

     S - Select Printer                      HP LaserJet Series II
     B - Binding Offset                      0"
     N - Number of Copies                    1
     U - Multiple Copies Generated by        WordPerfect
     G - Graphics Quality                    Medium
     T - Text Quality                        High

Selection: 0
```

The options on the Print menu are as follows:

- *Full Document.* Prints the entire document.
- *Page.* Prints the page the cursor is positioned on.

- *Document on Disk*. Enables you to print a file that is stored on disk. (To print selected pages from a file stored on disk, see the Multiple Pages discussion below.)

- *Control Printer*. Enables you to control the printer once you've directed WordPerfect to print. This option is described in more detail below.

- *Multiple Pages*. Enables you to print selected pages from a document. This option is described in more detail below.

- *View Document*. "Print" your document to the screen so you can see what it will look like when it is printed out.

- *Initialize Printer*. The **Initialize Printer** option enables you to load font (typeface and size) instructions into your printer's RAM so you can print in a variety of sizes and styles.

PRINTING MULTIPLE PAGES AND COPIES

WordPerfect provides a number of options for printing selective pages from a document. After initiating the PRINT command and choosing the Multiple Pages option, you can type in page numbers in any of the following patterns. (We use 3 and 5 to represent two page numbers.)

3	Prints page 3
3,5	Prints pages 3 and 5
3 5	Prints pages 3 and 5 (same as above)
3-5	Prints pages 3 through 5
3-	Prints the document beginning with page 3
-3	Prints from the beginning of the document to page 3

CONTROLLING THE PRINTER

When you initiate the command to print a document, WordPerfect refers to your request as a **print job**. Instead of making you wait while the document is printed, WordPerfect then passes control back to you so you can continue editing a document or selecting a document to print. What this means is that you can line up a series of print jobs to print, and then continue to work while WordPerfect prints them out.

The **Control Printer** option of the Print menu enables you to control your print jobs. After choosing the Control Printer option, the screen will look like Figure 4.12. The options on this menu are described as follows:

Figure 4.12

The Control Printer option of the Print menu has been chosen.

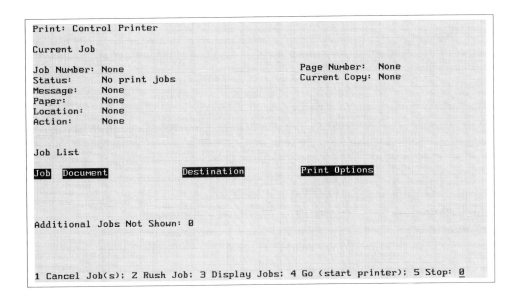

```
Print: Control Printer

Current Job

Job Number:  None                        Page Number:  None
Status:      No print jobs               Current Copy: None
Message:     None
Paper:       None
Location:    None
Action:      None


Job List

Job  Document                Destination        Print Options




Additional Jobs Not Shown: 0



1 Cancel Job(s); 2 Rush Job; 3 Display Jobs; 4 Go (start printer); 5 Stop: 0
```

- *Cancel Job(s).* Use this option to cancel the printing of one or more print jobs. To cancel the printing of a particular job, type the number of the print job, and then press (Enter). To cancel the printing of all print jobs, type *, and then choose Yes.

- *Rush Job.* This option lets you change the printing order of your print jobs. If you want one job to print before another, type the number of the job you want to rush and then press (Enter).

- *Display Jobs.* Choosing this option will list all the jobs you have selected to print.

- *Go (start printer).* Choose this option if you have previously paused the printer using the Stop option.

- *Stop.* This command enables you to pause the printer so that you can make adjustments to it. For example, you may need to change the print ribbon or remove a piece of paper that has gotten jammed.

PRINTING A BLOCK

Although the Print menu provides options for printing an entire document or selected pages from a document, it doesn't provide an option for printing a block of text. For example, you may just want to print a few paragraphs or a few sections from a document. To print a block of text, use the following procedure:

1. Position the cursor at the beginning of the block of text that you want to print.

2. To initiate the BLOCK command.
   PRESS: Alt+F4 (*or* F12)

3. Use the cursor-movement keys to highlight the block.

4. To print the block:
   PRESS: Shift+F7
   WordPerfect will display the prompt "Print block? No (Yes)".
   CHOOSE: Yes

Quick Reference
Printing a Block

1. To initiate the BLOCK command:
   PRESS: Alt+F4 (*or* F12)
2. Highlight the block that you want to print.
3. To print the block:
   PRESS: Shift+F7
   CHOOSE: Yes

GRAPHICS (Alt+F9)

The **GRAPHICS** command (Alt+F9) provides a number of command options that make it possible to produce reports, newsletters and other documents with graphics to enhance message clarity. *Using the menu bar, choose Graphics.* After initiating the GRAPHICS command, WordPerfect displays the menu pictured in Figure 4.13.

The GRAPHICS command provides many options. The main steps involved with including graphics in your documents include: (1) type your document text, (2) create an empty **graphic box**, which is an area in your document that is reserved for graphics, and (3) put text or a picture into the graphics box, which you can later resize and reposition to meet your needs.

To print a document that includes a graphic, you need to use a printer that is capable of printing graphics. In addition, your computer must be configured with a graphics display card if you want to use the View option within the Print menu to see on the screen how the document will appear when printed.

Figure 4.13

The Graphics
menu

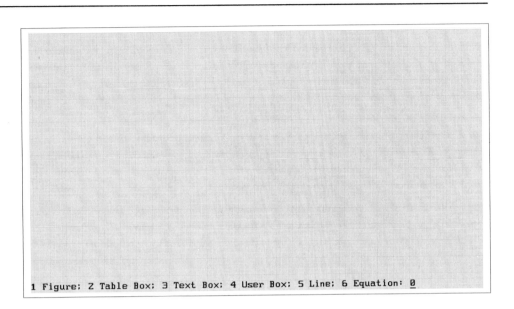

1 Figure; 2 Table Box; 3 Text Box; 4 User Box; 5 Line; 6 Equation: 0

GRAPHICS BOXES

WordPerfect lets you create four different types of empty graphics boxes (that you will later fill with something), each with different characteristics. Each type of graphics box is pictured in Figure 4.14.

- *Figure box.* A figure box is an empty box with a frame for a border

Figure 4.14

Graphics
boxes

Empty Table Box

Empty
Figure Box

Empty Text Box

Empty
User Box

- *Table box.* A table box has dark lines on the top and on the bottom .

- *Text box.* A text box is the same as a table box with shading.

- *User box.* A user box has no border or shading.

GRAPHICS BOX CONTENTS

Although their names suggest that you have to put figures in figure boxes and tables in table boxes, you can put any type of information into a box. The box name merely describes its characteristics when it is empty, and helps you to organize the different graphic elements in a document. In other words, you can put text into a figure box, and a table into a user box. Graphics boxes can contain figures, tables, and text.

- *Figures.* The graphic you see in Figure 4.15 is one of thirty that are packaged with WordPerfect. These graphics are stored in individual files on disk, and each file has the extension of WPG. In addition, if you want to create graphics using another program, WordPerfect provides a command that you can use to convert graphics files created by other programs into a graphics file format that WordPerfect can understand (that is, into a file with the extension of WPG).

Figure 4.15

Graphics. A graphic can be brought into a document using the GRAPHICS command (Alt+F9).

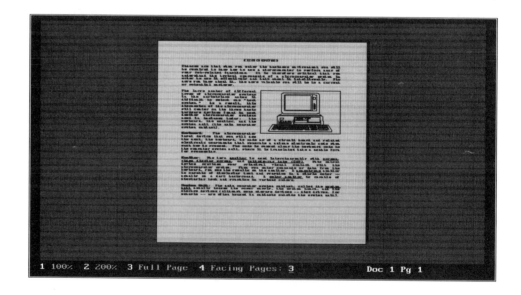

- *Tables.* Tables, which you learn how to create in Session 5, can be included in your documents with or without the use of a table box. The main reason you would want to use a table box is if you want text to wrap around the table in your document. (Note: You need to know how to create a table before you can create a box that creates a table.)

- *Text.* Text in a box is like text in a document. Text boxes are often used to emphasize quotations or statements.

CREATING A GRAPHICS BOX

The process of including a graphic in your document is simple and doesn't involve much more than retrieving the graphic from disk and inserting it at the current cursor position. In the steps below we lead you through creating the document pictured in Figure 4.15. You will begin by retrieving a file from the Advantage Diskette named WPMICRO. Perform the following steps:

1. Make sure the Advantage Diskette is in drive A:. Retrieve WPMICRO from the Advantage Diskette.

2. Position the cursor on the first character (T) of the second paragraph. This marks where you want to insert the graphic called PC-1.WPG.

3. To initiate the GRAPHICS command:
    PRESS: Alt + F9

4. Since you want to insert a graphics figure in your document:
    CHOOSE: Figure
    CHOOSE: Create

5. Since the graphics figure you are inserting is currently stored on the disk, you must choose the Filename option to tell WordPerfect what figure to retrieve:
    CHOOSE: Filename

6. To list the files on your WordPerfect disk and then highlight the PC-1.WPG file:
    PRESS: F5
    TYPE: C:
    PRESS: Enter
    (Note: If the name isn't listed, the graphics files may be stored in a different subdirectory. Ask your instructor or lab assistant.)
    PRESS: *the cursor-movement keys to search the list for PC-1.WPG. Highlight the file named PC-1.WPG. The screen should look like Figure 4.16.*

Figure 4.16

Listing the
graphics files
stored on
your disk

```
09-01-92  04:41p              Directory C:\WP51\GRAPHICS\*.*
Document size:    2,820   Free: 33,871,872 Used:    170,594     Files:     58

  CERTIF  .WPG      679  04-12-90 12:00p │ CHECK    .WPG   1,076  06-12-89 03:59p
  CHKBOX-1.WPG      653  04-12-90 12:00p │ CLOCK    .WPG   6,236  06-12-89 03:59p
  CNTRCT-2.WPG    2,753  04-12-90 12:00p │ CONFIDEN.WPG   3,228  06-12-89 03:59p
  DEVICE-2.WPG      657  04-12-90 12:00p │ DIPLOMA  .WPG   2,413  04-12-90 12:00p
  FLAG    .WPG      732  06-12-89 03:59p │ FLOPPY-2.WPG     475  04-12-90 12:00p
  GAVEL   .WPG      858  06-12-89 03:59p │ GLOBEZ-M.WPG   7,785  04-12-90 12:00p
  GOODNEWS.WPG    4,244  06-12-89 03:59p │ HAND     .WPG   1,056  06-12-89 03:59p
  HANDS-3 .WPG    1,117  04-12-90 12:00p │ HOURGLAS.WPG   1,836  06-12-89 03:59p
  KEY     .WPG    1,580  06-12-89 03:59p │ MAGNIF   .WPG   1,023  04-12-90 12:00p
  MAILBAG .WPG    3,353  04-12-90 12:00p │ MAPSYMBL.WPG   2,452  06-12-89 03:59p
  NEWS    .WPG    1,201  04-12-90 12:00p │ NEWSPAPR.WPG   1,390  06-12-89 03:59p
  NO1     .WPG    3,236  06-12-89 03:59p │ PC       .WPG   2,588  06-12-89 03:59p
  PC-1    .WPG    4,035  04-12-90 12:00p │ PENCIL   .WPG   3,512  06-12-89 03:59p
  PHONE   .WPG    4,182  06-12-89 03:59p │ PRESENT  .WPG   1,432  06-12-89 03:59p
  PRESNT-1.WPG    4,123  04-12-90 12:00p │ PRINTR-3.WPG   1,899  04-12-90 12:00p
  QUILL   .WPG    1,312  06-12-89 03:59p │ RPTCARD  .WPG   6,056  06-12-89 03:59p
  SCALE   .WPG    3,071  04-12-90 12:00p │ STAR-5   .WPG     391  04-12-90 12:00p
  TELPHONE.WPG    6,101  04-12-90 12:00p │ THINKER  .WPG   4,628  06-12-89 03:59p
  TROPHY  .WPG    3,891  04-12-90 12:00p │ USAMAP   .WPG   9,084  06-12-89 03:59p

 1 Retrieve; 2 Delete; 3 Move/Rename; 4 Print; 5 Short/Long Display;
 6 Look; 7 Other Directory; 8 Copy; 9 Find; N Name Search: 6
```

7. The cursor should be highlighting the file named PC-1.WPG. To retrieve this file:
   CHOOSE: Retrieve
   The Graphics menu should again be displaying on the screen. Note the option for Horizontal Position. As indicated on the menu, the graphic will be positioned on the right side of the page.

8. To return to the document and then cause the text to conform around the graphic:
   PRESS: F7
   To conform the text around the graphic:
   PRESS: ↓
   The screen should look similar to Figure 4.17. Note that you can see only the box that the graphic will be positioned in. You can see the actual graphic only if you print the document on the printer or view the document on the screen (using the View option within the Print menu).

9. At this point, if your computer is connected to a graphics printer, perform the following procedure to print:
   PRESS: Shift + F7
   CHOOSE: Full Document
   The printout should look like Figure 4.15. If your computer is configured with a graphics card, perform the following procedure to view the document on the screen:
   PRESS: Shift + F7
   CHOOSE: View Document
   The graphic should be displaying in the graphics box.
   PRESS: F7

Figure 4.17

Retrieving a
graphic into
a document. To
view the graphic,
you must print
the document or
use the View
option in the
Print menu.

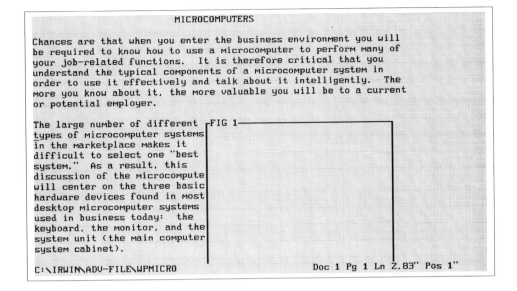

10. Save the document onto the Advantage Diskette as WPMICRO.4.

Quick Reference
Graphics
Alt + F9

To retrieve a graphic (that is stored on disk) into your document:
1. To initiate the GRAPHICS command:
   PRESS: Alt + F9
2. CHOOSE: Figure, Create, Filename
3. To list the graphics files, type c:, and then press Enter.
4. Highlight a file that has the extension of WPG.
5. To retrieve the highlighted file:
   CHOOSE: Retrieve
6. To return to the document:
   PRESS: F7
   To conform the text around the graphic:
   PRESS: ↓
7. To see the inserted graphic, use the View option within the Print menu or print the document out on the printer.

FILE MANAGEMENT COMMANDS (F5)

The LIST FILES (F5) command lists the files and subdirectories (if subdirectories exist) stored on a disk , and provides a number of options for managing files. *Using the menu bar, choose List Files from the Retrieve menu.*

When you first press (F5), WordPerfect will list the files in the current directory unless you type in a different disk and/or directory path. If you want to change the default directory, type = , and then type in the new directory information. After you press (Enter), WordPerfect will consider this new directory to be the current directory. As a result, the next time you list files, the files in this directory will be listed.

When you list the files stored on a disk, you have the following **file management commands** available to you:

- *Retrieve.* To retrieve a file into RAM, highlight the file with the cursor-movement keys and choose the Retrieve option. This option (described in Session 1) is especially useful when you have forgotten the name of the file you want to retrieve.

- *Delete.* To delete a file from the disk, highlight the file with the cursor-movement keys and choose the Delete option. WordPerfect will respond with "Delete filename? (Y/N)." Type Y to delete the file and N if you decide not to delete the file. To delete a group of files at once, you can mark each file with an asterisk and then choose the Delete option. To mark a file with an asterisk, highlight the file and then type an asterisk. (The asterisk will appear next to the filename.)

- *Move/Rename.* To rename a file, highlight it with the cursor-movement keys and choose the Rename option. Type the new filename. (WordPerfect won't allow you to use a name that already exists in the current directory.)

- *Print.* With this option, you can print a file by highlighting it and choosing the Print option. If you choose more than one file to print, WordPerfect will print them in sequence. (You can work on one document while another document is printing.)

- *Short/Long Display.* When this option is chosen, WordPerfect lists files using the long display rather than the short display. In the Long Display mode, only WordPerfect data files are listed on the screen. The files are listed by their descriptive name rather than by their filename. Also, the information for each file takes up one line. (In the Short Display mode, the information for two files is listed in a row.)

- *Look.* The text of the highlighted file is displayed on the screen. This command enables you to take a glimpse into a file (without retrieving it) if you forget what the contents of the file are.

- *Other Directory.* With this command, you can change the current disk or subdirectory to list the files stored on another disk or in another subdirectory.

- *Copy.* By choosing this option, you can make a copy of the highlighted file. If the copy will be stored in the current directory, you must provide a different name for the file. To copy a group of files at once, mark each file with an asterisk and then choose the Copy option. To mark a file, highlight the file and then type an asterisk. (The asterisk will appear next to the filename.)

- *Find.* Use this option to display those files in the current directory that meet certain search conditions. This option is useful if you're looking for a particular file but have no idea what its name is. For example, you might want to search for a file that contains the words "Department Budget." The files that meet your search condition will list on the screen. You can then use the Look option to display the contents of a particular file or retrieve the file.

- *Name Search.* Rather than highlighting a file using the cursor-movement keys (in the List Files menu), you can choose the Name Search option and type the name (or the first few characters) of the file you want to highlight.

SUMMARY

In this session you learned how to use commands to enhance the appearance of your printed documents. Each of these commands can be initiated by first positioning the cursor where you want the command to begin taking effect and then displaying the Format menu (Shift+F8). You learned how to change margins and the justification of a document. You also learned how to protect against widows and orphans, include page numbers, include a header or a footer, and include graphics in a document.

In addition, you learned how to perform file-management tasks using the LIST FILES command (F5).

COMMAND SUMMARY

The table on the next page provides a list of the commands and procedures covered in this session.

Table 4.1 Command Summary	(Shift)+(F8), Line, Margins, type a # that corresponds to a new margin, (Enter), (F7), (F7)	Change margins
	(Shift)+(F8), Line, Justification, choose an option, (F7)	Change justification to left, full, or centered
	(Shift)+(F8), Line, Widow/Orphan Protection, choose Yes or No, (F7)	Widow/Orphan protection
	(Shift)+(F8), Page, Page Numbering, Page Number Position, choose a positioning option, (F7)	Include page numbers in a document
	(Shift)+(F8), Page, choose Header or Footer, choose an option, choose a positioning option, type the header/footer text, (F7), (F7)	Include headers/footers in a document
	(Alt)+(F4), highlight the block, (Shift)+(F7), Yes	Print a block
	(Alt)+(F9), Figure, Create, Filename, type c:, (Enter), highlight a file, Retrieve, (F7)	Include a graphics figure in a document

KEY TERMS

Control Printer   In WordPerfect, this command enables you to control the printer once you've directed it to print.

file-management commands   In WordPerfect, these commands enable you to perform such tasks as copying, deleting, and renaming files.

footer   Descriptive information (such as a page number and date) that appears at the bottom of each page of a document.

Graphics ((Alt)+(F9))   In WordPerfect, this command enables you to include graphic elements in a document.

graphics box   In WordPerfect, this is an area in your document reserved for graphics.

header   Descriptive information (such as page number and date) that appears at the top of each page of a document.

Initialize Printer This WordPerfect printing option enables you to load font (typeface and size) instructions into your printer's RAM so you can print in a variety of sizes and styles.

justification In word processing, the activity of aligning words along the margin as centered, left-aligned, or right-aligned.

New Page Number Using this WordPerfect command, you can specify what page number will print on the current page. Unless specified, the physical page number will print.

orphan The first line of a paragraph that begins on the last line of a page.

Page Number Style This WordPerfect command can be used to customize the way the page number appears on the page.

print job When you initiate the command to print a document, WordPerfect refers to your request as a print job.

widow The last line of a paragraph that begins on the first line of a page.

EXERCISES

SHORT ANSWER

1. What is the purpose of invoking widow/orphan protection?
2. What is a graphics box?
3. What is the View Document option of the Print menu used for?
4. The Page Numbering option (within the FORMAT command) offers what flexibility relating to where page numbers appear on the printed page?
5. What does it mean to change the justification of a document?
6. What are the hardware requirements for using the GRAPHICS command?
7. In the LIST FILES command, what capability does the Find option provide?
8. What steps are involved with printing a block?
9. What is a print job?
10. In the LIST FILES command, what capability does the Look option provide?

HANDS-ON

1. Retrieve SOFTWARE.4 from the Advantage Diskette. Perform the following steps:
   a. Include a header that displays the current date in the flush-right position.
   b. Protect against widows and orphans.
   c. Left justify the entire document.
   d. Include your name and the current page number in a footer.
   f. Spell-check the document.

    g. Save SOFTWARE.4 onto the Advantage Diskette.

    h. Print SOFTWARE.4.

2. Use the LIST FILES command (F5) to list the files on the Advantage Diskette. To practice using the LIST FILES command, perform the following tasks:

    a. Highlight the file named SOFTWARE.4. Make a copy of this file onto the Advantage Diskette. Name the copy SOFTCOPY.4.

    b. Rename the SOFTCOPY.4 file to DOCUMENT.4.

    c. Use the LOOK command to display the text in the SALES.MAR file on the screen. Remember that this option only allows you to take a glimpse into the file; you can't edit the file unless you retrieve it. Press the Exit key (F7) when you're finished looking at the file.

    d. You should still be viewing the List Files screen. Print the entire DOCUMENT.4 file.

    e. Delete the DOCUMENT.4 file.

    f. Exit the List Files menu so that you are viewing the document screen.

3. This exercise practices using some commands from previous sessions, as well as document formatting commands:

    a. Clear the screen.

    b. Set the following margin specifications:

Top Margin	1.5"
Bottom Margin	1.5"
Left Margin	2"
Right Margin	2"

    c. Create a header that has `P&L Projection, 1993` in the left-aligned position and `Page ^B` in the right-aligned position.

    d. Create a footer that has `*** Confidential ***` in the left-aligned position and `By your name` in the right-aligned position.

    e. Create the document pictured below:

```
                        ABC REALTY, INC.


                                                             1993

           Revenue
                Commercial Properties          125,500,000
                Residential Properties          35,000,000
                Leased Properties                  875,000

           Total Revenue                       $161,375,000

           Expenses
                Insurance                           50,000
                Salaries                           750,000
                Commissions                     15,500,000
                Office Supplies                     25,000
                Office Equipment                    20,000
```

```
Utilities                    15,000
Leased Automobiles           50,000
Travel                      250,000
Advertising & Promotion  25,000,000

Total Expenses           41,660,000

Net Income            $119,115,000
```

   f. Save the document as ABCPROJ onto the Advantage Diskette.

   g. Print ABCPROJ.

4. This exercise practices creating a two-page document that includes headers and footers (the first page is a title page). Perform the following steps:

   a. Clear the screen.

   b. Type the following text into the first page of the document (the title page):

     PRESS: Enter *ten times*

     TYPE: BUDGET FORECAST

     PRESS: Enter *twice*

     TYPE: 1993

     PRESS: Enter *ten times*

     TYPE: ABC REALTY, INC.

     PRESS: Enter *twice*

     TYPE: Sales Team

     PRESS: Enter *four times*

     TYPE: Prepared By: *your name*

   c. Center all the text on this page by first highlighting it with the BLOCK command and then using the CENTER command.

   d. To force a page break:

     PRESS: Ctrl + Enter

   e. At the top of the second page, enter the text pictured below:

```
Introduction

Now that we are in the first quarter of 1993, it
is time we stopped to review our direction for
the remainder of the year. We had a tough year
in 1992, but it seems that the economy is well
on its way to recovery. We are anticipating a
good year for all the staff.

This report is confidential and should not be
circulated outside of this office. It is
intended to be a planning document for the Sales
Team in 1993. Any questions or suggestions can
be directed to your immediate supervisor.
```

f. Position the cursor at the top of the second page.

g. Include the following text in the footer:
    `copyright 1993 ABC Realty, Inc.`

h. Include the page number in a header. The header should be right-aligned and look like the following: `Page ^B`

i. Save this document as 1993ABC onto the Advantage Diskette.

5. Look in the Job Opportunities section of your local newspaper and make a list of the types of jobs that require experience using microcomputers. Note: Don't include the jobs that require the experience of a computer professional who has been educated in the technical aspects of computers. Do many jobs require microcomputer experience? What types of software are important to know how to use? Create a two-page document on this topic and then add the following:

a. Widow/orphan protection.

b. Page numbering in the bottom-center of each page.

c. A header that prints on both pages and includes your name.

d. A header that prints on both pages and includes the current date (remember, WordPerfect lets you include two headers in a document).

e. A code in the document that turns justification off.

f. If possible, include a graphic in your document (try to choose a graphic that will enhance the topic of your document).

g. In addition, include underlining, boldfacing, centering, indenting, and double-spacing.

h. Spell-check the document.

i. Save this document onto the Advantage Diskette and give the document the name of your choice.

j. Print the document.

SESSION 5

ADVANCED FEATURES

In this session, you will use WordPerfect to create tables and columns, print form letters, create macros, and generate outlines.

PREVIEW

When you have completed this session, you will be able to:

Create tables.
·
Create newspaper-style and parallel columns.
·
Perform a merge procedure to generate form letters.
·
Use macros to automate procedures.
·
Create outlines.

Why Is This Session Important?
Table Fundamentals
> Creating a Table
> Resizing a Column
> Entering Text
> Other Editing Features

Newspaper-Style Columns
> Defining Newspaper-Style Columns
> Turning the COLUMN Command On and Off
> Editing Newspaper-Style Columns

Parallel Columns
> Defining, Using, and Editing Parallel Columns

Merging Fundamentals
> Creating a Primary File (Shift+F9)
> Creating a Secondary File
> Merging the Primary and the Secondary File (Ctrl+F9)

Macros
> Creating a Macro (Ctrl+F10)
> Using a Macro (Alt+F10)

Outline (Shift+F5)
Summary
> Command Summary

Key Terms
Exercises
> Short Answer
> Hands-On

WHY IS THIS SESSION IMPORTANT?

In this session, you learn how to create tables, newspaper-style columns, and parallel columns. In addition, you learn how to automate some WordPerfect operations. You will automate the procedure of sending the same letter (called a *form letter*) to different people by using the MERGE command. And you will learn how to use the MACRO command to automate other procedures, such as changing the line spacing or margins in a document. In addition, you will learn how to automate the procedure of creating outlines.

Before proceeding, make sure the following are true:

1. You have access to WordPerfect 5.1.

2. Your Advantage Diskette is inserted in the drive. You will save your work onto the diskette and retrieve the files that have been created for you. (Note: The Advantage Diskette can be made by copying all the files off your instructor's Master Advantage Diskette onto a formatted diskette.)

TABLE FUNDAMENTALS

A **table** is composed of columns and rows and is usually part of another document. The table feature can be used to create a **basic table** (Figure 5.1), which contains rows and columns of uniform size, and **parallel columns** (Figure 5.2), which are commonly used for documents that contain rows and columns of different sizes, such as a meeting schedule or résumé.

WordPerfect refers to the intersection of a column and a row as a **cell** and gives each cell in your table a name (Figure 5.3). The columns in a table are named A, B, C, and so on. The rows in a table are named 1, 2, 3, and so on. The cell in the upper-left corner of a table is referred to as cell A1, and the cell to its right is referred to as cell B1. Likewise, the cells below cell B1 are referred to as cell B2, B3, B4, and so on.

After defining the number of columns and rows you want to include in a table, you can resize the columns and rows in order to create parallel columns. In addition, as shown in Figure 5.4, you can perform other editing features such as shading selected cells, inserting or deleting columns and rows, joining or splitting cells, or removing the lines in a table.

Figure 5.1

A basic
table. The
rows and
columns are
of uniform
size.

8 - 9	Blue Room	Orientation.
9 - 10	Green Room	Staff members.
10 - 10:15	Staff Lounge	Break - coffee.
10:15 - Noon	Executive Offices	Zoo Committee.
Noon - 1:00	Walrus Pond	Awards Luncheon.
1:00 - 3:30	Lion's Den	Zoo Tour.■

Cell C6 Doc 1 Pg 1 Ln 2.54" Pos 6.33"

Figure 5.2

Parallel col-
umns. The
rows and
columns are
different sizes.

MEETING SCHEDULE
JUNE 8, 1993

8 - 9	Blue Room	Orientation Meeting for new volunteers. Familiarize new volunteers with overall objectives of the zoo and the rules and regulations booklet.
9 - 10	Green Room	Staff Member Meeting. Focus of session is on the rules and regulations of the zoo.
10 - 10:15	Staff Lounge	Break - coffee
10:15 - Noon	Executive Offices	Meeting of the Zoo Committee. Strategy session for the 1994 season.
Noon - 1:00	Walrus Pond	Awards Luncheon
1:00 - 3:30	Lion's Den	Zoo Tour. Familiarize volunteers with the rules the public must adhere to when around the animals. It's the job of the volunteers to enforce the rules.

CREATING A TABLE

In this section you will create the schedule pictured in Figure 5.2 using the
TABLE command (Alt+F7). *Using the menu bar, choose Tables from the
Layout menu.*

Figure 5.3

The inter-
section of a
row and col-
umn in a table
is referred to
as a cell.

```
        Column A              Column B              Column C

   This is cell A1.

                                              This is cell C2.

                         This is cell B3.

   This is cell A4.




                                         Doc 1 Pg 1 Ln 1.33" Pos 1"
```

Figure 5.4

This schedule
was created
using the
TABLE
command.

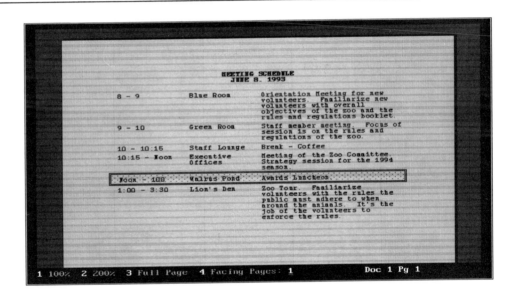

Perform the following steps:

1. Clear the screen.
    PRESS: F7
    CHOOSE: No, No

2. First, as pictured in Figure 5.2, center and boldface the following titles:
    MEETING SCHEDULE
    JUNE 8, 1993

3. After typing in the titles:
    PRESS: (Enter) *twice*
    The cursor is now located where you want the table to be positioned.

4. To initiate the TABLE command:
    PRESS: (Alt)+(F7)
    CHOOSE: Tables, Create

5. WordPerfect is now displaying a prompt relating to the number of columns you want displayed in the table. Unless you specify otherwise, WordPerfect will create a table with 3 columns. Since this assumption is fine:
    PRESS: (Enter)

6. Wordperfect is now displaying a prompt relating to the number of rows you want displayed in the table. To complete the table pictured in Figure 5.2, you need 6 rows.
    TYPE: 6
    PRESS: (Enter)
    The screen should look like Figure 5.5. WordPerfect is now in Table Edit mode. In this mode, you can change the characteristics of the table. For example, you can widen/narrow columns or insert/delete columns. In the next section you will narrow the first two columns of the table.

Figure 5.5

The number of columns and rows have been defined, and WordPerfect is in Table Edit mode.

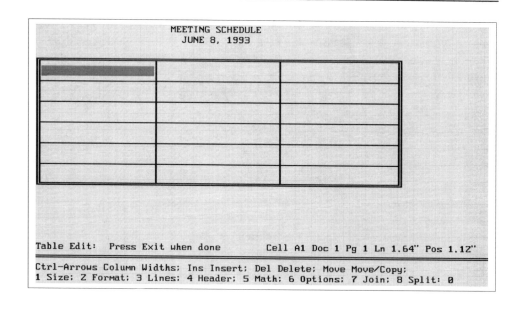

Quick Reference
Creating a Table
[Alt]+[F7]

To insert a table in your document:
1. Position the cursor where the table should be positioned, and then initiate the TABLE command:
   PRESS: [Alt]+[F7]
2. CHOOSE: Tables, Create
3. TYPE: *a number that corresponds to how many columns you want included in the table*
   PRESS: [Enter]
4. TYPE: *a number that corresponds to how many rows you want included in the table*
   PRESS: [Enter]

RESIZING A COLUMN

To widen or narrow a table column, WordPerfect must first be in Table Edit mode. To widen a column, position the cursor in the column to be widened, and then press [Ctrl]+[→] until the column is the desired width. Likewise, to narrow a column, position the cursor in the column to be narrowed, and then press [Ctrl]+[←] until the column is the desired width.

If you look at Figure 5.2, you can see that the first two columns (columns A and B) aren't as wide as the third column (column C). In the next few steps, you will narrow the first two columns and widen the third column.

1. The cursor should be positioned in column A, which is the column you want to narrow. To narrow the column:
   PRESS: [Ctrl]+[←] *six times*

2. To narrow column B, first position the cursor in column B and then narrow the column:
   PRESS: [→]
   PRESS: [Ctrl]+[←] *six times*

3. To widen column C, first position the cursor in column C and then widen the column.
   PRESS: [→]
   PRESS: [Ctrl]+[→] *twelve times*
   The screen should look like Figure 5.6.

Figure 5.6

Columns A, B, and C have been widened using [Ctrl]+ [→].

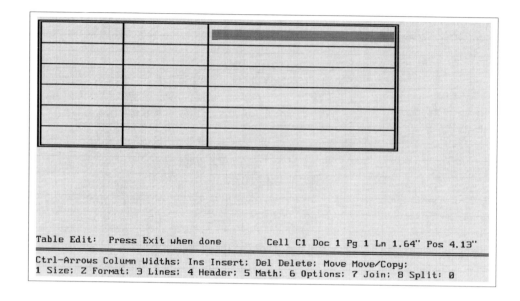

```
Table Edit:   Press Exit when done          Cell C1 Doc 1 Pg 1 Ln 1.64" Pos 4.13"
Ctrl-Arrows Column Widths; Ins Insert; Del Delete; Move Move/Copy;
1 Size; 2 Format; 3 Lines; 4 Header; 5 Math; 6 Options; 7 Join; 8 Split: 0
```

4. To position the cursor back in cell A1:
    PRESS: [←] *twice*

5. To exit Table Edit mode so you can fill in the table:
    PRESS: [F7]
    WordPerfect is now waiting for you to type in the table information.

6. To be safe, save your work now onto the Advantage Diskette as TABLE.ZOO:
    PRESS: [F10]
    TYPE: A:TABLE.ZOO
    PRESS: [Enter]

....

Quick Reference
Widening or
Narrowing a Column
in a Table

To widen or narrow a column in a table:
1. Make sure WordPerfect is in Table Edit mode ([Alt]+[F7], Tables, Edit).
2. Position the cursor in the column to be widened or narrowed.
3. Press [Ctrl]+[→] to widen the column or [Ctrl]+[←] to narrow the column.

....

ENTERING TEXT

In this section you will type the text pictured in Figure 5.2 into the table. You can move from cell to cell in the table using the [←], [→] (or [Tab]), [↑], and [↓] keys. Once you've typed text into a cell, *don't* press [Enter]. Pressing [Enter] will increase the height of the row. If the text you type is too wide to fit in a cell,

WordPerfect will automatically increase the height of the cell to accommodate the text.

Perform the following steps to fill in the first row of the table:

1. Position the cursor in cell A1.

2. With the cursor in cell A1:
    TYPE: 8 - 9
    PRESS: [→]

3. The cursor should now be positioned in cell B1.
    TYPE: Blue Room
    PRESS: [→]

4. The cursor should now be positioned in cell C1.
    TYPE: Orientation Meeting for new volunteers. Familiarize new volunteers with overall objectives of the zoo and the rules and regulations booklet.

5. To position the cursor in cell A2 so you can fill in the second row of the table:
    PRESS: [↓]
    PRESS: [←] *twice*
    The screen should look like Figure 5.7.

Figure 5.7

Data has been entered into the first row of the table.

```
                        MEETING SCHEDULE
                         JUNE 8, 1993

 ┌─────────┬────────────┬──────────────────────────────┐
 │ 8 - 9   │ Blue Room  │ Orientation Meeting for new  │
 │         │            │ volunteers. Familiarize new  │
 │         │            │ volunteers with overall      │
 │         │            │ objectives of the zoo and the│
 │         │            │ rules and regulations booklet.│
 ├─────────┼────────────┼──────────────────────────────┤
 │ -       │            │                              │
 ├─────────┼────────────┼──────────────────────────────┤
 │         │            │                              │
 ├─────────┼────────────┼──────────────────────────────┤
 │         │            │                              │
 ├─────────┼────────────┼──────────────────────────────┤
 │         │            │                              │
 └─────────┴────────────┴──────────────────────────────┘
```

C:\IRWIN\DISKETTE\TABLE.ZOO   Cell A2 Doc 1 Pg 1 Ln 2.59" Pos 1.12"

---

6. Refer to Figure 5.2 to fill in the rest of the table. Remember *not* to press [Enter] after filling in a cell. To move the cursor to an adjacent cell, use the cursor keys.

7. Save (and replace) your work now onto the Advantage Diskette as TABLE.ZOO.

8. Print TABLE.ZOO:
    PRESS: (Shift)+(F7)
    CHOOSE: Full Document
    The printout should look like Figure 5.2.

OTHER EDITING FEATURES

The procedures described in the following sections can be used to customize a table to meet your needs.

SHADING CELLS

The procedure of shading cells is used to emphasize certain cells in a table (Figure 5.4). In Figure 5.4, the luncheon activities are shaded. The shading procedure is described below:

1. Move the cursor to a cell in the table, and then initiate the TABLE command.

2. Move the cursor to the cell you want to shade. If you want to shade more than one cell, use the BLOCK command now to highlight the cells to be shaded.

3. CHOOSE: Lines, Shade, On

INSERTING ROWS AND COLUMNS

After creating a table, you may decide that you need to include an additional column or row in the table. The procedure of inserting rows and columns in a table is described below:

1. Move the cursor to a cell in the table, and then initiate the TABLE command.

2. Move the cursor to where you want to insert a column or row.

3. PRESS: (Insert)

4. Choose Rows or Columns from the menu.

5. To insert just one row or column, press (Enter). Otherwise, type a number that corresponds to the number of rows or columns to be inserted.

DELETING ROWS AND COLUMNS

After creating a table, you may decide that a particular column or row isn't necessary. The procedure for deleting rows and columns in a table is as follows:

1. Move the cursor to a cell in the table, and then initiate the TABLE command.

2. Move the cursor to the column or row that you want to delete.

3. PRESS: (Delete)

4. Choose Rows or Columns from the menu.

5. To delete just one row or column, press (Enter). Otherwise, type a number that corresponds to the number of rows or columns to be deleted.

JOINING CELLS

After creating a table, you may decide to join two or more cells to create a larger cell. The procedure for joining cells is as follows:

1. Move the cursor to a cell in the table, and then initiate the TABLE command.

2. Highlight the cells to be joined using the BLOCK command.

3. CHOOSE: Join

SPLITTING CELLS

After creating a table, you may decide to split two or more cells to create smaller cells. The procedure for splitting cells is as follows:

1. Move the cursor to a cell in the table, and then initiate the TABLE command.

2. Move the cursor to the cell you want to split, or highlight more than one cell using the BLOCK command.

3. CHOOSE: Split

4. Choose Rows or Columns from the menu.

5. Type a number that corresponds to the number of cells to split the selected cells into.

EDITING TABLE LINES

After creating a table, you may decide to edit the lines in a table. For example, you may want to change the width of the lines or delete the lines. In Figure 5.4, all lines have been deleted. The procedure of editing the lines in a table is described below:

1. Move the cursor to a cell in the table, and then initiate the TABLE command.

2. To change the lines of a single cell, move the cursor to that cell. To change the lines of more than one cell, use the BLOCK command now to highlight the cells to be changed.

3. CHOOSE: Lines

4. Choose an option from the menu that is currently displaying. This menu lets you specify what lines to edit from the selected cells.

5. Choose an option from the menu that is currently displaying. Using this menu you can specify the width of the selected line(s) or that no lines display.

NEWSPAPER-STYLE COLUMNS

Newspaper-style columns (Figure 5.8) are often used in promotional material such as a flier, newsletter, or report. Text in newspaper columns flows down the left side of the page until it reaches the bottom, and then wraps up to the top of the next column. If there are only two columns on the page, the text will then begin flowing down the left side of the next page.

Figure 5.8

Newspaper-style columns

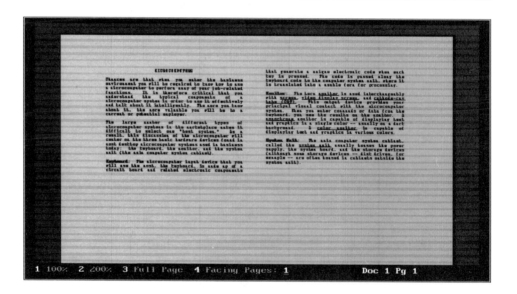

Creating newspaper columns involves four steps:

1. Define the characteristics of the newspaper columns using the COLUMN command ((Alt)+(F7)) and then choose Define. *Using the menu bar, choose Columns from the Layout menu, and then choose Define.* Specify that you want to create Newspaper columns, the number of columns that you want to display on a page, and how wide each column should be.

2.   Position the cursor where you want the column specifications to begin taking effect, and then turn the COLUMN command on by choosing On after initiating the COLUMN command. *Using the Menu bar, choose Columns from the Layout menu, and then choose On.* If you already have text in a document that you want to display in columns, position the cursor at the beginning of the text to be affected.

3.   Type in the text that you want to display in columns. If you have already typed in the text, position the cursor at the end of the text that you want displayed in columns.

4.   Turn the COLUMN command off by choosing Off after initiating the COLUMN command. *Using the menu bar, choose Columns from the Layout menu, and then choose Off.* When you are done typing in the text that you want displayed in columns, or have positioned the cursor at the end of the text to be displayed in columns, turn the COLUMN command off.

DEFINING NEWSPAPER-STYLE COLUMNS

In this section you will define the characteristics of the newspaper-style columns that you want to include in a document. You will retrieve a document named WPMICRO.

CAUTION: When defining columns, the cursor *must* be somewhere above the text that you will want to display in columns. (WordPerfect will insert a code in your document that represents the column definition, and this code must be above the cursor when you turn the COLUMN command on.)

Perform the following steps:

1.   Retrieve WPMICRO from the Advantage Diskette.

2.   Make sure the cursor is positioned at the top of the document.

3.   To initiate the COLUMN command:
     PRESS: Alt + F7
     CHOOSE: Columns, Define
     The screen should look like Figure 5.9. Unless you make a change on this screen, WordPerfect will display 2 newspaper columns in your document (after you turn the COLUMN command on) and they will each be 3 inches wide. At this point, you can change any of the specifications.

Figure 5.9

Defining news-
paper-style
columns

```
Text Column Definition

  1 - Type                              Newspaper

  2 - Number of Columns                 2

  3 - Distance Between Columns

  4 - Margins

  Column  Left    Right   Column  Left    Right
    1:    1"      4"        13:
    2:    4.5"    7.5"      14:
    3:                      15:
    4:                      16:
    5:                      17:
    6:                      18:
    7:                      19:
    8:                      20:
    9:                      21:
   10:                      22:
   11:                      23:
   12:                      24:

Selection: 0
```

4. Since you want to include two newspaper columns in the document, you don't need to change any of these column definitions. To exit back to your document:
   PRESS: F7 *twice*

5. WordPerfect has just inserted a column definitions code in your document. To see the code:
   PRESS: Alt+F3
   This column definition will be in effect for any columns that are created after this code in the document.
   PRESS: Alt+F3

CAUTION: The cursor must first be above the text that will be put into columns when defining the column specifications.

In the next step you will turn the COLUMN command on so you can see the column definition at work.

Quick Reference
Defining News-
paper Style
Columns

To define newspaper-style columns:
1. Initiate the COLUMNS command:
   PRESS: Alt+F7
2. CHOOSE: Columns, Define
3. TYPE: *a number that corresponds to how many columns you want included in the document*
   PRESS: Enter
4. PRESS: F7 *twice*

TURNING THE COLUMN COMMAND ON AND OFF

After defining the specifications for the columns, you must then turn the COLUMN command on in order to use the specifications. Perform the following steps:

1. Position the cursor at the beginning of the first paragraph.

2. To turn the COLUMN command on:
    PRESS: Alt+F7
    CHOOSE: Columns, On

3. To display the document in 2 columns:
    PRESS: ↓
    The screen should look like Figure 5.10.

Figure 5.10

The COLUMN command has been initiated.

```
                          MICROCOMPUTERS

Chances are that when you enter     monochrome monitor is capable
the business environment you        of displaying text and graphics
will be required to know how to     in a single color — usually on
use a microcomputer to perform      a dark background.  A color
many of your job-related            monitor is capable of
functions.  It is therefore         displaying text and graphics in
critical that you understand        various colors.
the typical components of a
microcomputer system in order       System Unit:  The main computer
to use it effectively and talk      system cabinet, called the
about it intelligently.  The        system unit usually houses the
more you know about it, the         power supply, the system board,
more valuable you will be to a      and the storage devices
current or potential employer.      (although some storage devices
                                    — disk drives, for example —
The large number of different       are often housed in cabinets
types of microcomputer systems      outside the system unit).
in the marketplace makes it
difficult to select one "best
system."  As a result, this
discussion of the microcomputer
will center on the three basic
C:\IRWIN\ADV-FILE\WPMICRO                Col 1 Doc 1 Pg 1 Ln 1.5" Pos 1"
```

---

4. To view the entire document:
    PRESS: Shift+F7
    CHOOSE: View
    The whole document is now displaying in two columns.
    PRESS: F7

5. Save WPMICRO as WPMICRO.5.

Quick Reference
Turning the COLUMN
Command On/Off

1. After including the column definition in your document, position the cursor where the COLUMN command should begin taking effect.
   PRESS: Alt + F7
2. CHOOSE: Columns, On
3. TYPE: *the text to be formatted into columns or position the cursor at the end of the text to be formatted into columns*
4. CHOOSE: Columns, Off

EDITING NEWSPAPER-STYLE COLUMNS

At first, it may seem a bit tricky to edit data that you have displayed in columns. You need to know the specific techniques for moving the cursor from column to column. These procedures are as follows:

- To move the cursor up and down in a column, use ↑ and ↓.

- To move the cursor left and right in a column, use ← and →.

- To move the cursor from a column on the left to a column on the right, press Ctrl + Home, and then →.

- To move the cursor from a column on the right to a column on the left, press Ctrl + Home, and then ←.

- To move the cursor to the right-most column on a page, press Ctrl + Home, Home, and then →.

- To move the cursor to the left-most column on a page, press Ctrl + Home, Home, and then ←.

When editing the text displayed in a column, WordPerfect automatically formats the text to conform to the column definition.

CAUTION: Even after you've mastered the cursor-movement techniques necessary to edit column data, you may find that WordPerfect is unforgiving at times. To avoid a frustrating experience, we recommend that you type the text that you want to display in columns and edit it *before* you turn the COLUMN command on.

PARALLEL COLUMNS

Whereas newspaper-style columns are best when creating columns that are the same width and that contain text that flows from one column to the next, **parallel columns** are useful when creating documents that involve columns of different sizes and that contain blocks of text, such as a résumé or a schedule sheet. Figure 5.11 pictures a document that uses parallel columns.

The TABLE command, described at the beginning of this session, is actually easier to use and provides more capabilities for creating parallel columns. However, if you are already accustomed to creating newspaper-style columns and haven't yet used the TABLE command, you may be inclined to use the COLUMN command instead.

Figure 5.11

Parallel columns. This document was created using the COLUMN command.

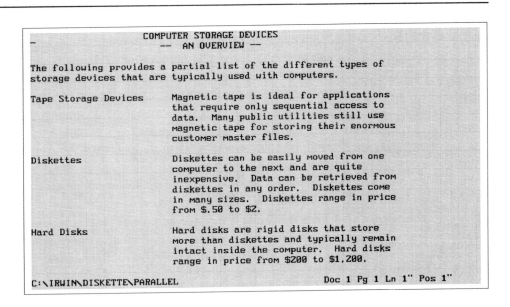

```
                     COMPUTER STORAGE DEVICES
                        -- AN OVERVIEW --
     The following provides a partial list of the different types of
     storage devices that are typically used with computers.

     Tape Storage Devices        Magnetic tape is ideal for applications
                                 that require only sequential access to
                                 data.  Many public utilities still use
                                 magnetic tape for storing their enormous
                                 customer master files.

     Diskettes                   Diskettes can be easily moved from one
                                 computer to the next and are quite
                                 inexpensive.  Data can be retrieved from
                                 diskettes in any order.  Diskettes come
                                 in many sizes.  Diskettes range in price
                                 from $.50 to $2.

     Hard Disks                  Hard disks are rigid disks that store
                                 more than diskettes and typically remain
                                 intact inside the computer.  Hard disks
                                 range in price from $200 to $1,200.

     C:\IRWIN\DISKETTE\PARALLEL                  Doc 1 Pg 1 Ln 1" Pos 1"
```

The basic steps for creating parallel columns, described below, are the same as for creating newspaper-style columns.

1. Define the characteristics of the parallel columns using the COLUMN command (Alt+F7),and then choose Define. *Using the menu bar, choose Columns from the Layout menu, and then choose Define.* Specify that you want to create Parallel columns, the number of columns that you want to display on a page, and how wide each column should be.

2. Position the cursor where you want the column specifications to begin taking effect, and then turn the COLUMN command on by choosing On after initiating the COLUMN command. *Using the Menu bar, choose Columns from the Layout menu, and then choose On.* If you already have text in a

document that you want to display in columns, position the cursor at the beginning of the text to be affected.

3. Type in the text that you want to display in columns. After you type information into one column, press Ctrl + Enter to move the cursor into the adjacent column. If you have already typed in the text, position the cursor at the end of the text that you want displayed in columns.

4. Turn the COLUMN command off by choosing Off after initiating the COLUMN command. *Using the menu bar, choose Columns from the Layout menu, and then choose Off.* When you are done typing in the text that you want displayed in columns, or have positioned the cursor at the end of the text to be displayed in columns, turn the COLUMN command off.

DEFINING, USING, AND EDITING PARALLEL COLUMNS

Defining the characteristics of parallel columns is very similar to defining the characteristics of newspaper-style columns. Make sure that the cursor is somewhere above the text that you will want to display in parallel columns. (WordPerfect will insert a code in your document that represents the column definition, and this code must be above the cursor when you turn the COLUMN command on.)

In the following steps we describe defining and then using parallel columns:

1. To initiate the COLUMN command:
    PRESS: Alt + F7
    CHOOSE: Define

2. To specify parallel columns:
    CHOOSE: Type
    Additional options should be displaying on the bottom of the screen (Figure 5.12).
    CHOOSE: Parallel
    If you select Parallel with Block Protect, WordPerfect won't break up any part of a block displaying in the parallel column if the cursor reaches the end of the page. Instead, it will move the entire block to the next page.

3. At this point, as necessary, you can specify how many columns you want to display, and how wide you want each column to be. When finished, press F7.

4. When you're ready to format text into parallel columns, position the cursor where you want the column definition to take effect, turn Column Mode on using the COLUMN command, and then choose On. When you're finished formatting text into columns, turn the COLUMN command off.

Figure 5.12

The Text Column Definition menu. The Type option has been chosen.

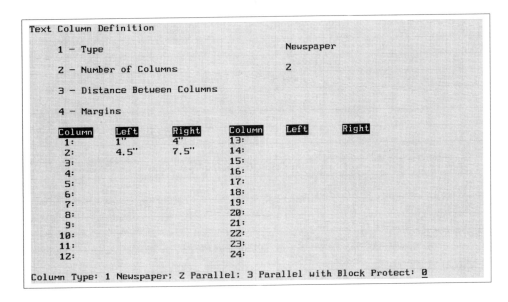

```
Text Column Definition

   1 - Type                              Newspaper

   2 - Number of Columns                 2

   3 - Distance Between Columns

   4 - Margins

   Column  Left    Right   Column  Left    Right
     1:    1"      4"        13:
     2:    4.5"    7.5"      14:
     3:                      15:
     4:                      16:
     5:                      17:
     6:                      18:
     7:                      19:
     8:                      20:
     9:                      21:
    10:                      22:
    11:                      23:
    12:                      24:

Column Type: 1 Newspaper; 2 Parallel; 3 Parallel with Block Protect: 0
```

When editing parallel columns, follow the procedures used to edit newspaper columns.

MERGING FUNDAMENTALS

You probably have received letters in the mail (even from organizations you've never heard of) with your name typed at the top of the letter, in the salutation, and maybe even in the middle of a paragraph. What you received was a form letter. Your name, along with hundreds of others, is part of a data file, and the names in this data file were automatically placed into the letter in predetermined locations through a process called **merging.** Merging involves the use of two files. The body of the letter is referred to as the **document file** (or **primary file** as WordPerfect calls it). The **data file** (or **secondary file**) contains all of the variable data (such as names and addresses) to be included in the document file in the merging process.

When creating a secondary file, you must define the *records* that you want to store in the file. For example, if you are sending a letter to potential employers, the data for each employer is referred to as a *record*. Each record is made up of *fields*. For example, each employer record might contain name, title, address, city, state, and zip fields. In the primary file, you need to put field codes in the file to indicate what field data (from the secondary file) should be inserted at that location during the merge process.

CREATING A PRIMARY FILE ([Shift]+[F9])

In this section you will retrieve the letter pictured in Figure 5.13 from the Advantage Diskette. Then you will modify it so that it can be used as the primary file in a merge. The **MERGE CODES** command is used to prepare the primary file to receive information from the secondary file.

1.   Retrieve SEMINAR.LET from the Advantage Diskette.

2.   Edit the letter to include your name at the bottom (as indicated in the letter).

Figure 5.13

SEMINAR.LET

```
February 27, 1993


Ms. Donna Abrahamson
355 Walnut Street
San Francisco, CA 94109

Dear Ms. Abrahamson:

I hear you're in the medical profession!  You could benefit very
much by attending my free seminar on health and fitness.  It will
be offered at Sporting Life, on 123 Main Street in Boston.  Ms.
Abrahamson, if you are interested please call Sporting Life to set
up a reservation.

Hope to hear from you soon!


(your name)



C:\IRWIN\ADV-FILE\SEMINAR.LET                        Doc 1 Pg 1 Ln 1" Pos 1"
```

Figure 5.14

SEMINAR.LET with inserted merge codes. Each merge code refers directly to the corresponding field in a secondary (data) file.

```
February 27, 1993



{FIELD}1~ {FIELD}2~ {FIELD}3~
{FIELD}4~
{FIELD}5~

Dear {FIELD}1~ {FIELD}3~:

I hear you're in the {FIELD}6~ profession!  You could benefit very much by
attending my free seminar on health and fitness.  It will be
offered at Sporting Life, on 123 Main Street in Boston.  {FIELD}1~ {FIELD}3~, if
you are interested please call Sporting Life to set up a
reservation.

Hope to hear from you soon!


(your name)



C:\IRWIN\ADV-FILE\SEMINAR.LET                        Doc 1 Pg 1 Ln 1" Pos 1"
```

Perform the following steps to edit the document so that it looks like Figure 5.14.

To substitute the appropriate merge code for "Ms." (Field 1) at the top of the letter:

1. Position the cursor beneath the "M" of "Ms."

2. To choose the MERGE CODES command:
   PRESS: Shift + F9
   CHOOSE: Field
   To specify Field 1:
   TYPE: 1
   PRESS: Enter

3. To delete "Ms.":
   PRESS: Del *three times*

To substitute the appropriate merge code for "Donna" (Field 2):

1. Position the cursor beneath the "D" of "Donna."

2. To choose the MERGE CODES command:
   PRESS: Shift + F9
   CHOOSE: Field
   To specify Field 2:
   TYPE: 2
   PRESS: Enter

3. To delete "Donna":
   PRESS: Del *five times*

To substitute the appropriate merge code for "Abrahamson" (Field 3):

1. Position the cursor beneath the "A" of "Abrahamson."

2. To choose the MERGE CODES command:
   PRESS: Shift + F9
   CHOOSE: Field
   To specify Field 3:
   TYPE: 3
   PRESS: Enter

3. To delete "Abrahamson":
   PRESS: Del *ten times*

To substitute the appropriate merge code for "355 Walnut Street" (Field 4):

1. Position the cursor beneath the "3" of "355 Walnut Street"

2. To choose the MERGE CODES command:
    PRESS: (Shift)+(F9)
    CHOOSE: Field
    To specify Field 4:
    TYPE: 4
    PRESS: (Enter)

3. To delete "355 Walnut Street":
    PRESS: (Del) *until the address is deleted*

To substitute the appropriate merge code for "San Francisco, CA 94109" (Field 5):

1. Position the cursor beneath the "S" of "San Francisco, CA 94109"

2. To choose the MERGE CODES command:
    PRESS: (Shift)+(F9)
    CHOOSE: Field
    To specify Field 5:
    TYPE: 5
    PRESS: (Enter)

3. To delete "San Francisco, CA 94109":
    PRESS: (Del) *until the city, state, and zip code information is deleted*

To substitute the appropriate merge code for "Ms." in the salutation:

1. Position the cursor beneath the "M" of "Ms.".

2. To choose the MERGE CODES command:
    PRESS: (Shift)+(F9)
    CHOOSE: Field
    To specify Field 1:
    TYPE: 1
    PRESS: (Enter)

3. To delete "Ms.":
    PRESS: (Del) *three times*

To substitute the appropriate merge code for "Abrahamson" in the salutation:

1. Position the cursor beneath the "A" of "Abrahamson".

2. To choose the MERGE CODES command:
    PRESS: ⁅Shift⁆+⁅F9⁆
    CHOOSE: Field
    To specify Field 3:
    TYPE: 3
    PRESS: ⁅Enter⁆

3. To delete "Abrahamson":
    PRESS: ⁅Del⁆ *ten times*

To substitute the appropriate merge code for "medical" (Field 6) in the first sentence:

1. Position the cursor beneath the "m" of "medical".

2. To choose the MERGE CODES command:
    PRESS: ⁅Shift⁆+⁅F9⁆
    CHOOSE: Field
    To specify Field 6:
    TYPE: 6
    PRESS: ⁅Enter⁆

3. To delete "medical":
    PRESS: ⁅Del⁆ *seven times*

To substitute the appropriate merge code for "Ms." (Field 1) in the last sentence:

1. Position the cursor beneath the "M" of "Ms."

2. To choose the MERGE CODES command:
    PRESS: ⁅Shift⁆+⁅F9⁆
    CHOOSE: Field
    To specify Field 1:
    TYPE: 1
    PRESS: ⁅Enter⁆

3. To delete "Ms.":
    PRESS: ⁅Del⁆ *three times*

To substitute the appropriate merge code for "Abrahamson" (Field 3):

1. Position the cursor beneath the "A" of "Abrahamson"

2. To choose the MERGE CODES command:
    PRESS: $\boxed{\text{Shift}} + \boxed{\text{F9}}$
    CHOOSE: <u>F</u>ield
    To specify Field 3:
    TYPE: 3
    PRESS: $\boxed{\text{Enter}}$

3. To delete "Abrahamson":
    PRESS: $\boxed{\text{Delete}}$ *ten times*
    Don't worry if the right margins appear to be out of alignment. When printed, each letter will be aligned.

4. Save this document onto the Advantage Diskette as SEMINAR.LET.

....

Quick Reference
Creating a Primary
File: $\boxed{\text{Shift}} + \boxed{\text{F9}}$

To insert a merge code in your document:
1. Initiate the MERGE CODES command:
    PRESS: $\boxed{\text{Shift}} + \boxed{\text{F9}}$
2. CHOOSE: <u>F</u>ield
3. TYPE: *a field number*
    PRESS: $\boxed{\text{Enter}}$

....

CREATING A SECONDARY FILE

To create a secondary (data) file using WordPerfect, you must follow a specific format. In WordPerfect, every field must be followed by an {END FIELD} code, and all records in the file must be separated by an {END RECORD} code. The {END FIELD} codes are put into the secondary file by pressing $\boxed{\text{F9}}$; the {END RECORD} codes are put in by pressing $\boxed{\text{Shift}} + \boxed{\text{F9}}$ and then choosing the End Record option.

Figure 5.15 shows the secondary file you will create. You will save it onto the Advantage Diskette as WPDATA. Although most secondary files contain many records, there are only three records in this file.

1. First, make sure you have saved SEMINAR.LET onto the Advantage Diskette.

2. Clear RAM using the following procedure:
    PRESS: $\boxed{\text{F7}}$
    CHOOSE: <u>N</u>o, <u>N</u>o

Figure 5.15

WPDATA
secondary file.
This data file
contains three
records of infor-
mation that will
be merged into
the primary
file called
SEMINAR.LET.

```
Ms.{END FIELD}
Patricia{END FIELD}
Stephens{END FIELD}
1992 Winding Way{END FIELD}
Chicago, Illinois 60637{END FIELD}
law{END FIELD}
{END RECORD}
================================================================================
Mr.{END FIELD}
Jack{END FIELD}
Yee{END FIELD}
392 Riverbend Drive{END FIELD}
Chicago, Illinois 60637{END FIELD}
medical{END FIELD}
{END RECORD}
================================================================================
Ms.{END FIELD}
Dalila{END FIELD}
Fernandez{END FIELD}
3621 Rothwell Court{END FIELD}
Chicago, Illinois 60637{END FIELD}
engineering{END FIELD}
{END RECORD}
================================================================================
Field: 1                                        Doc 1 Pg 1 Ln 1" Pos 1"
```

To create the file named WPDATA, perform the following steps:

3. To enter the first record:
    TYPE: Ms.
    PRESS: (F9)
    TYPE: Patricia
    PRESS: (F9)
    TYPE: Stephens
    PRESS: (F9)
    TYPE: 1992 Winding Way
    PRESS: (F9)
    TYPE: Chicago, Illinois 60637
    PRESS: (F9)
    TYPE: law
    PRESS: (F9)
    To enter the {END RECORD} code before adding another record:
    PRESS: (Shift)+(F9)
    CHOOSE: End Record

4. To enter the second record:
    TYPE: Mr.
    PRESS: (F9)
    TYPE: Jack
    PRESS: (F9)
    TYPE: Yee
    PRESS: (F9)
    TYPE: 392 Riverbend Drive
    PRESS: (F9)
    TYPE: Chicago, Illinois 60637
    PRESS: (F9)

TYPE: medical
PRESS: F9
To enter the {END RECORD} code before adding another record:
PRESS: Shift+F9
CHOOSE: End Record

5. To enter the third record:
TYPE: Ms.
PRESS: F9
TYPE: Dalila
PRESS: F9
TYPE: Fernandez
PRESS: F9
TYPE: 3621 Rothwell Court
PRESS: F9
TYPE: Chicago, Illinois 60637
PRESS: F9
TYPE: engineering
PRESS: F9
To enter the {END RECORD} code before adding another record:
PRESS: Shift+F9
CHOOSE: End Record

6. Save this document onto the Advantage Diskette as **WPDATA**.

Quick Reference
Creating a Secondary File: Shift+F9

1. To clear RAM of any data:
   PRESS: F7
   CHOOSE: No, No
2. TYPE: *field data*
   PRESS: F9
3. Repeat Step 2 until all field data has been entered.
4. After typing all the data in for a record, you must insert the {END RECORD} code:
   PRESS: Shift+F9
   CHOOSE: End Record
5. Repeat Steps 2—4 until all records have been entered.

MERGING THE PRIMARY FILE AND THE SECONDARY FILE (Ctrl+F9)

The process for merging a primary file and a secondary file is as follows:

• Clear RAM of any data (F7, No, No).

- Initiate the **MERGE/SORT** command ([Ctrl]+[F9]).

- Type the disk drive designation and name of the primary file (SEMINAR.LET).

- Type the disk drive designation and name of the secondary file (WPDATA).

Perform the following steps to merge SEMINAR.LET with WPDATA:

1. If data is on the screen, clear it by doing the following:
   PRESS: [F7]
   CHOOSE: <u>N</u>o, <u>N</u>o

2. To initiate the MERGE/SORT command and choose the Merge option:
   PRESS: [Ctrl]+[F9]
   CHOOSE: <u>M</u>erge

3. WordPerfect is now prompting you to enter the disk drive designation and name of the primary file.
   TYPE: A:SEMINAR.LET
   PRESS: [Enter]

4. WordPerfect is now prompting you to enter the name of the secondary file.
   TYPE: A:WPDATA
   PRESS: [Enter]

You should now see the message "** Merging **" in the bottom left-hand corner of the screen. When the merge is complete, your cursor is positioned at the end of all the merged documents. To see the documents, press [PgUp]. Note that the names and addresses were replaced by the names and addresses in your data file, and the profession data was merged into the first line of the letter. In addition, Field 1 and Field 3 were merged into the last line of the letter.

Now that the merging process is complete, you have a few options: (1) if you want to view the letters on paper, print them out; (2) save the letters onto a data diskette and print them later; or (3) clear RAM and merge the two files later.

MACROS

Macros are used to automate frequently used procedures. For example, if you always type the same text (such as the name and address of the company you're working for) into multiple documents, you can use a macro to automate the procedure of typing in the text. Or, if you often find it necessary to make the same formatting changes in your documents, such as a line spacing or tab line change, you can automate these procedures with a macro. In the sections below you learn how to create and use macros.

Quick Reference
Merging
Ctrl + F9

1. To clear RAM of any data:
    PRESS: F7
    CHOOSE: No, No
2. To initiate the MERGE command:
    PRESS: Ctrl + F9
    CHOOSE: Merge
3. TYPE: *the disk drive designation and the name of the primary file*
    PRESS: Enter
4. TYPE: *the disk drive designation and the name of the secondary file*

CREATING A MACRO (Ctrl + F10)

The procedure of creating a macro involves the following:

*   Initiate the **MACRO DEFINE** command (Ctrl + F10).

*   Type a name for the macro.

*   Type a macro description.

*   Perform the procedure you want to automate.

*   Turn the MACRO DEFINE command off (Ctrl + F10).

Perform the following steps to create a macro named WPBEGIN that automates the procedure of typing the letterhead information, current date, and salutation of a letter.

1. To clear RAM:
    PRESS: F7
    CHOOSE: No, No

2. To initiate the MACRO DEFINE command:
    PRESS: Ctrl + F10

3. The text "Define Macro:" should display in the bottom left-hand corner of the screen. WordPerfect is waiting for you to assign a name to the macro.

TYPE: A:WPBEGIN
PRESS: [Enter]

4. WordPerfect is now waiting for you to type in a description for the macro.
TYPE: Letter Beginning
PRESS: [Enter]

5. The text "Macro Def" should be blinking in the lower left-hand corner. Every keystroke you type now will be stored in the macro until you turn the MACRO DEFINE command off ([Ctrl]+[F10]). If you make mistakes while typing, correct them as you normally would.

To type in the letterhead information (you will boldface and center the letterhead information in the next two steps after typing it in):
PRESS: [Caps]
TYPE: SPORTING LIFE
PRESS: [Enter]
TYPE: 129 STRIDING WAY
PRESS: [Enter]
TYPE: CHICAGO, ILLINOIS 60637
PRESS: [Enter]

To boldface the letterhead information:
PRESS: *cursor-movement keys until the cursor is beneath the "S" of "Sporting Life"*
PRESS: [Alt]+[F4]
PRESS: [Enter] *three times (to highlight the letterhead information)*
PRESS: [F6]

To center the letterhead information:
PRESS: *cursor-movement keys until the cursor is beneath the "S" of "Sporting Life"*
PRESS: [Alt]+[F4]
PRESS: [Enter] *three times (to highlight the letterhead information)*
PRESS: [Shift]+[F6]
TYPE: Y

To enter the current date and salutation:
PRESS: [Caps]
PRESS: [Enter] *three times*
PRESS: [→] *once to move the cursor to the right of the bold code (so the date doesn't appear boldfaced)*
PRESS: [Shift]+[F5]
CHOOSE: Date Text
PRESS: [Enter] *four times*
TYPE: Dear

To turn the MACRO DEFINE command off:
PRESS: [Ctrl]+[F10]
The macro has now been saved onto the Advantage Diskette. WordPerfect automatically supplied the extension of WPM to your macro name (WPBEGIN.WPM).
To clear RAM:
PRESS: [F7]
CHOOSE: No, No

Quick Reference
Creating a Macro
[Ctrl]+[F10]

1. To initiate the MACRO DEFINE command:
   PRESS: [Ctrl]+[F10]
2. TYPE: *a macro filename (don't supply an extension)*
   PRESS: [Enter]
3. TYPE: *a few words to describe the macro*
   PRESS: [Enter]
4. Perform the procedure you want to automate.
5. To turn the MACRO command off:
   PRESS: [Ctrl]+[F10]

USING A MACRO ([Alt]+[F10])

In this section you will use the WPBEGIN.WPM macro. Make sure the screen is cleared before performing the following procedure.

1. To initiate the **MACRO** command:
   PRESS: [Alt]+[F10]

2. The text "Macro:" should display in the bottom left-hand corner. WordPerfect is waiting for you to type in the name of the macro you want to use.
   TYPE: A:WPBEGIN
   PRESS: [Enter]

The screen should look like Figure 5.16. If you can't see the top of the letterhead, press [PgUp].

Figure 5.16

Using the WP-BEGIN macro. This is what will appear on the screen after executing the WPBEGIN macro. To execute a macro, use Alt+F10.

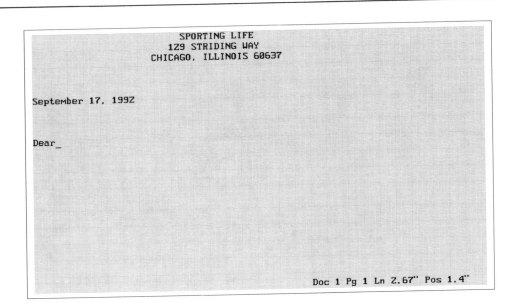

```
                        SPORTING LIFE
                       129 STRIDING WAY
                    CHICAGO, ILLINOIS 60637


September 17, 1992


Dear_
```
Doc 1 Pg 1 Ln 2.67" Pos 1.4"

Quick Reference
Using a Macro
Alt+F10

1. To initiate the MACRO command:
   PRESS: Alt+F10
2. Type a macro name and then press Enter.

OUTLINE (Shift+F5)

The **OUTLINE** command (Shift+F5) makes it easy to create outlines, which are commonly used to help organize topics that relate to a particular subject. As shown in Figure 5.17, an outline is composed of levels. WordPerfect automatically represents the first level with a Roman numeral (for example, I). The second level is represented with capital letters (for example, A), and the third level is represented with numbers (for example, 1). The fourth level is represented with lowercase letters (for example, a).

In this section we lead you through creating the outline pictured in Figure 5.17. Once you initiate the OUTLINE command, you will press Enter to begin typing the first level of the outline. WordPerfect will automatically supply "I" to mark the first level. After typing in the first level, you will press Enter. At this point you can either begin typing at this same level, or press Tab to begin typing at a new level. Press Shift+Tab to type at a previous level.

Figure 5.17

The OUTLINE document. This document was created using the OUTLINE command.

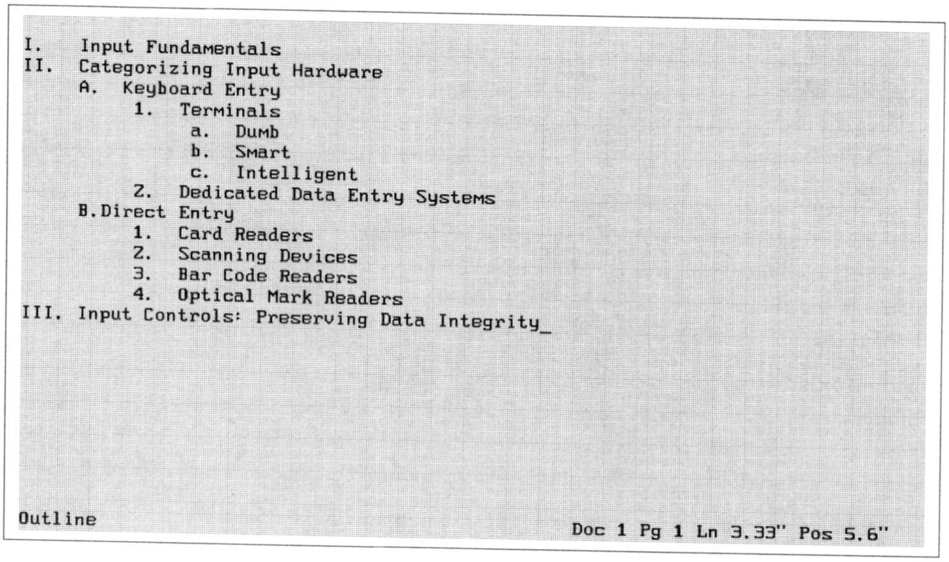

```
I.    Input Fundamentals
II.   Categorizing Input Hardware
      A.  Keyboard Entry
          1.   Terminals
               a.   Dumb
               b.   Smart
               c.   Intelligent
          2.   Dedicated Data Entry Systems
      B.Direct Entry
          1.   Card Readers
          2.   Scanning Devices
          3.   Bar Code Readers
          4.   Optical Mark Readers
III.  Input Controls: Preserving Data Integrity_




Outline                                          Doc 1 Pg 1 Ln 3.33" Pos 5.6"
```

Perform the following steps to create the outline pictured in Figure 5.17:

1. Clear RAM of any data:
    PRESS: F7
    CHOOSE: No, No

2. To initiate the OUTLINE command:
    PRESS: Shift+F5

3. CHOOSE: Outline, On
    The word "Outline" should be displaying in the bottom-left corner of the screen. To begin the first level of the outline:
    PRESS: Enter

4. Roman numeral "I" should be displaying against the left margin. So that the text doesn't appear directly next to the number:
    PRESS: Space Bar *three times*
    TYPE: Input Fundamentals
    PRESS: Enter

5. Roman numeral "II" should be displaying against the left margin. So that the text doesn't appear directly next to the number, and so that the text appears lined up beneath the heading above:
    PRESS: Space Bar *twice*
    TYPE: Categorizing Input Hardware
    PRESS: Enter

6. To display a sublevel in the outline:
   PRESS: Tab
   The screen should now look like Figure 5.18.

Figure 5.18

Using the OUT-
LINE command.
To display a new
outline level, press
Tab. To display
a previous level,
press Shift +
Tab.

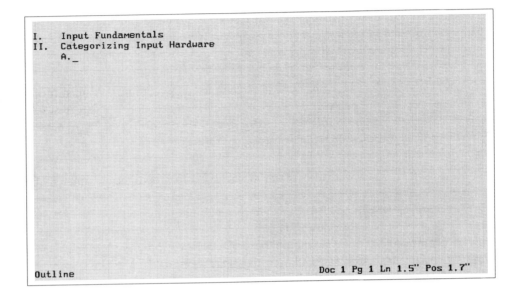

```
I.    Input Fundamentals
II.   Categorizing Input Hardware
      A. _




Outline                                    Doc 1 Pg 1 Ln 1.5" Pos 1.7"
```

PRESS: Space Bar *twice*
TYPE: Keyboard Entry
PRESS: Enter

7. To create the third level:
   PRESS: Tab
   PRESS: Space Bar *twice*
   TYPE: Terminals
   PRESS: Enter

8. To type the text into the fourth level:
   PRESS: Tab
   PRESS: Space Bar *twice*
   TYPE: Dumb
   PRESS: Enter
   PRESS: Space Bar *twice*
   TYPE: Smart
   PRESS: Enter
   PRESS: Space Bar *twice*
   TYPE: Intelligent
   PRESS: Enter

9. To type in the "Dedicated Data Entry Systems" text:
   PRESS: [Shift]+[Tab]
   PRESS: Space Bar *twice*
   TYPE: Dedicated Data Entry Systems
   PRESS: [Enter]

10. Complete the rest of the outline by referring to Figure 5.17. *Remember to press* [Tab] *to begin typing at a new level and* [Shift]+[Tab] *to begin typing at a previous level.*

11. When you have completed the outline, you must turn the OUTLINE command off:
    PRESS: [Shift]+[F5]
    CHOOSE: Outline, Off

12. Save the outline as OUTLINE onto the Advantage Diskette.

Quick Reference
Creating an Outline
[Shift]+[F5]

1. To initiate the OUTLINE command:
   PRESS: [Shift]+[F5]
   CHOOSE: Outline, On
   PRESS: [Enter]
   TYPE: *the heading for the current level*
   PRESS: [Enter]
2. To type the heading for a new level:
   PRESS: [Tab]
   TYPE: *the heading for the next level*
   PRESS: [Enter]
3. To type the heading for a previous level:
   PRESS: [Shift]+[Tab]
4. When you have completed the outline:
   PRESS: [Shift]+[F5]
   CHOOSE: Outline, Off

SUMMARY

This session introduced you to some advanced features of WordPerfect. You learned how to create tables, newspaper-style columns, parallel columns, and outlines. In addition, you learned how to use WordPerfect's automated mail merge feature, which enables you to easily send out customized form letters. The process of merging takes information from a data file, called the *secondary file*, and inserts it into the correct locations in the document file, called the *primary file*.

Another productivity tool, called *macros*, was also introduced in this session. Macros allow you to automate repetitive tasks that require several keystrokes. With macros, you can perform multiple tasks using only a few keystrokes.

COMMAND SUMMARY

The following table provides a list of the commands and procedures covered in this session.

Table 5.1 Command Summary	(Alt)+(F7), Tables, Create, type a # for columns, (Enter), type a # for rows, (Enter)	Create a table
	(Alt)+(F7), Tables, Edit, press (Ctrl)+(→) to widen a column or (Ctrl)+(←) to narrow a column	Resizing a column in a table
	(Alt)+(F7), Columns, Define, type a # for the columns, (Enter), (F7), (F7)	Define columns
	(Alt)+(F7), Columns, choose On or Off	Turning the COLUMN command On and Off
	(Shift)+(F9), Field, type a field number, (Enter)	Creating a primary file
	Type field data, (F9), continue until all field data is entered, (Shift)+(F9), End Record	Creating a secondary file
	(Ctrl)+(F9), Merge, type primary filename, (Enter), type secondary filename, (Enter)	Merging a primary and secondary file
	(Ctrl)+(F10), type a macro filename, (Enter), type a few words to describe the macro, perform the procedure to be automated, (Ctrl)+(F10)	Creating a macro

Table 5.1

Command Summary (concluded)

Alt+F10, type a macro filename, Enter		Using a macro
Shift+F5, Outline, On, Enter, type heading for current level, Enter, press Tab to type data at a new level or Shift+Tab to type data at a previous level until the outline is completed, Shift+F5, Off		Creating an outline

KEY TERMS

basic table A table that is composed of columns and rows of uniform size.

cell The intersection of a column and a row in a table. The cell at the intersection of column C and row 2 is cell C2.

data file In WordPerfect, the data file contains all the variable data (such as names and addresses) to be included in the document file in the **merging** process.

document file In WordPerfect, the document file contains the body of the letter into which data in the **data file** is inserted during the **merging** process.

macro A Collection of procedures and/or text created by the user and saved to disk, then used repeatedly to save time.

Macro (Alt+F10) The WordPerfect option used to execute a **macro**.

Macro Define (Ctrl+F10) The WordPerfect option used to collect the procedures to be stored in a macro file.

merging The process of merging a **document file** and **data file** together.

Merge Codes (Shift+F9) The WordPerfect option used to enter merge codes into a document to prepare it for the **merging** process.

Merge/Sort (Ctrl+F9) The WordPerfect option used to initiate the merging process.

newspaper-style columns A word processing feature that involves text flowing from one column to the next.

Outline (Shift+F5) A WordPerfect option used to make it easier to go through the process of creating an outline.

parallel columns A word processing feature that is useful when a document uses columns of different sizes that contain blocks of text, such as a résumé.

primary file   See **document file**.

secondary file   See **data file**.

table   A word processing feature that is composed of rows and columns and is usually part of another document.

Table (Alt+F7)   The WordPerfect option used to create **tables**.

EXERCISES

SHORT ANSWER

1. What steps must be followed to create a macro?
2. What are the rules for creating a secondary file?
3. What is the meaning of the term *merging*?
4. What steps are required to merge two files together?
5. How are Enter and Tab used when an outline is being created?
6. What do you think would be a good use for a macro (for example, to automatically format a document)?
7. What advantages does using the OUTLINE command provide over creating an outline without use of this command?
8. What would a good reason be to use the MERGE command?
9. Why is it a good idea to clear RAM before executing a merge?
10. What must you do to a document in order to prepare it for a merge?

HANDS-ON

1. In this exercise you will merge a primary and secondary file together to generate form letters.
   a. Retrieve the file named WPMERGE from the Advantage Diskette.
   b. Modify this letter so that it contains the appropriate field codes for the following data elements (make sure to include the code for Field 4 in the first sentence of the document):
      (1) Field 1—the manager's title.
      (2) Field 2—the manager's first name.
      (3) Field 3—the manager's last name.
      (4) Field 4—the name of the sporting goods store.
      (5) Field 5—the store's address.
      (6) Field 6—the city, state, and zip of the store.
   c. Include the current date at the top of the document.
   d. Substitute your name in place of the text "(your name)" at the bottom of the document.
   e. Save WPMERGE onto the Advantage Diskette.

    f.   Clear the contents of RAM (F7, <u>N</u>o, <u>N</u>o).

    g.   In this step you will create a secondary file named DATAFILE.WP that will be used shortly in a merge. By referring to Step c above, create a secondary file (data file) that contains five records. (As indicated in Step 1, each record contains six fields.)

    h.   Save this data onto the Advantage Diskette as DATAFILE.WP.

    i.   Clear RAM of any data and then merge WPMERGE and DATAFILE.WP together.

    j.   Print the merged documents.

2.   Using the OUTLINE command, create an outline of a course you are currently taking, planning to take, or wish were offered at your school. Save the outline onto the Advantage Diskette as OUTLINE.5. If the outline takes up more than one page, include a footer that reads:

```
COURSE OUTLINE -   ^B
```

(Remember that ^ represents pressing Ctrl and that ^B causes the current page number to appear when the document is printed.)

3.   The objective of this exercise is to create a macro that automates a routine procedure. Pretend you are in charge of keeping track of sales at a local sporting goods store. At the end of each day you have to type summary comments about sales activity for the current day. Create a macro named GETREADY that can be used to automate the procedure of getting ready to type these comments. The macro should do the following:

    a.   Change the spacing in your document to double-spacing.

    b.   Protect against widows/orphans.

    c.   Use the DATE command to insert the current date in the top left-hand corner of the page.

    d.   Create a footer that reads:
```
PAGE -   ^B
```

    e.   Move the cursor down a few lines and insert a centered title that reads:
```
DAILY SALES REPORT
```

    f.   Move the cursor down a few lines so you can begin typing.
Execute the macro.
Print the macro.

4.   In this exercise you will practice creating and formatting a table. Perform the following steps:

    a.   Create the document pictured on the following page:

current date

Mr. Roland Garros
Clay Supplies Inc.
1091 Panorama Ridge
Waco, TX 76798

Dear Mr. Garros:

Per your request, I am providing a list of the
items that you ordered for your office last
Wednesday.

Please confirm each item with a check mark in
the appropriate column and fax this letter back
to me at 817-747-1234.

Yours sincerely,
Grand Slam Computer Sales

your name
Account Representative

b. Insert the following table between the first and second paragraphs.

Client Initial	Qty	Description	Total Price
	5	Laser Printers	$10,250.00
	5	Printer Cables	76.00
	20	3.5" Diskettes	30.00
	5	Microsoft Windows	450.00

c. Save the document as ROLAND onto the Advantage Diskette.
d. Print ROLAND.

5. In this exercise you will create a primary file and a secondary file that you can use in a merge.
    a. Create the primary file (pictured on the next page) and save it onto the Advantage Diskette as CUSTFORM. *Where indicated, remember to insert the appropriate merge codes.*
    b. Create the secondary file (pictured on the next page) and save it onto the Advantage Diskette as CUSTDATA.
    c. Clear the screen and then merge the CUSTFORM and CUSTDATA files together.

today's date

<<GIVEN>><<SURNAME>>
<<ADDRESS>>
<<CITY>>, <<STATE>>   <<ZIP>>

Dear <<GIVEN>>:

                    We're moving!

Please be informed that as of August 31, 1993 we
are moving to new premises located at #250 -
8030 United Boulevard in Boston, MA.

We are looking forward to this move with great
anticipation. Because of your continued support,
we are expanding our training facilities to
accommodate two training rooms and a board room.

As a result of this move, we will be closed
starting from the third week in August to the
end of September. An invitation to the Open
House will be forwarded to you, **<<GIVEN>>**, as
soon as we are settled.

Let us know if we can do anything for you!

Sincerely,

your name
President

Given	Surname	Address	City	State	Zip
Elliot	Lepinski	898 Burrard Avenue	Louisville	KY	40205
Red	Robinson	235 Johnson Street	Washington	DC	20052
Elaine	Maynard	#701-1005 West 9th	Baton Rouge	LA	70803
Ranjitt	Singh	1227 E. Cordova	Tacoma	WA	98416
Jackson	Mor	36 Primore Road	Witchita	KS	67208
William	Delaney	875 Broadway	Albuquerque	NM	87131
Alice	Chan	29 Redmond Road	San Francisco	CA	92182
Jessie	Thomas	909 West 18th Srcet	Brooklyn	NY	11225
Jimmy	Kazo	888 East 8th Avenue	Billings	MT	59101